BIBLIOGRAPHIC RESOURCES FOR

A Confession of Faith
A Call to Action

THE CAPE TOWN COMMITMENT
A Confession of Faith, a Call to Action

Copyright © 2013 Darrell Bock / The Lausanne Movement. All rights reserved. Except for brief quotations in critical publications or reviews, no part of this book may be reproduced in any manner without prior written permission from the publisher. Write: Permissions, Wipf and Stock Publishers, 199 W. 8th Ave., Suite 3, Eugene, OR 97401.

Wipf & Stock
An Imprint of Wipf and Stock Publishers
199 W. 8th Ave., Suite 3
Eugene, OR 97401

www.wipfandstock.com

ISBN 13: 978-1-62564-003-1

Produced in the United States of America

A RESOURCE FROM:

www.lausanne.org
info@lausanne.org

BIBLIOGRAPHIC RESOURCES FOR
The Cape Town Commitment

CONTENTS

Introduction 5

Unit 1
   Preamble 9
   The Historical Context of *The Cape Town Commitment* 9
   Lausanne I (Lausanne, Switzerland) 1974 9
   Lausanne II (Manila, Philippines) 1989 10
   Lausanne III (Cape Town, South Africa) 2010 10
      [Referred to formally as The Third Lausanne Congress on World Evangelization]

PART 1: THE CAPE TOWN CONFESSION OF FAITH

Unit 2
   PART 1 • SECTION 1: God's Love 13

Unit 3
   PART 1 • SECTION 2: Our Love for God 15

Unit 4
   PART 1 • SECTION 3-5: God as Father, Son and Spirit 19
   PART 1 • SECTION 4: The Father 19
   PART 1 • SECTION 5: The Son 21
   PART 1 • SECTION 6: The Holy Spirit 23
   PART 1 • SECTION 3-5: The Trinity 25

Unit 5
   PART 1 • SECTION 6: Our Love for the Word 27
   PART 1 • SECTION 7: Our Love for the World 28

Unit 6
   PART 1 • SECTION 8: The Gospel 29
   PART 1 • SECTION 9: Our Love for God's People 31
   PART 1 • SECTION 10: Global Mission 32

PART 2: THE CAPE TOWN CALL TO ACTION

Unit 7
   PART 2 • SECTION IIA-1: Truth and the Person of Christ 35
   PART 2 • SECTION IIA-2: Truth and the Challenge of Pluralism 37
   PART 2 • SECTION IIA-3: The Workplace 40
   PART 2 • SECTION IIA-4: The Media 44
   PART 2 • SECTION IIA-5: The Arts 45
   PART 2 • SECTION IIA-6: Science and Technology 48
   PART 2 • SECTION IIA-7: Public Arenas 49

Contents

Unit 8
- Part 2•Section IIB-1: Reconciliation — 51
- Part 2•Section IIB-1A: Reconciliation, Peace and Jewish Evangelism — 52
- Part 2•Section IIB-2: Ethnic Conflict — 54
- Part 2•Section IIB-3: Slavery and Human Trafficking — 56
- Part 2•Section IIB-3A: Poverty — 58
- Part 2•Section IIB-4: People with Disabilities — 61
- Part 2•Section IIB-5: HIV/AIDS — 62
- Part 2•Section IIB-6: Stewardship and Creation — 65

Unit 9
- Part 2•Section IIC-1: People of Other Faiths — 67
- Part 2•Section IIC-2: Suffering — 70
- Part 2•Section IIC-3: Grace — 71
- Part 2•Section IIC-4: Discipleship — 72
- Part 2•Section IIC-5: Diaspora (Scattered Peoples) — 75
- Part 2•Section IIC-5A: Scattered Peoples - International Students — 77
- Part 2•Section IIC-6: Religious Freedom — 79

Unit 10
- Part 2•Section IID-1: Unreached People Groups — 81
- Part 2•Section IID-2: Orality — 83
- Part 2•Section IID-3: Christ-Centered Leadership — 87
- Part 2•Section IID-3A: Evangelism & Christian Leadership — 88
- Part 2•Section IID-4: Cities — 90
- Part 2•Section IID-5: Children — 92
- Part 2•Section IID-6: Evangelism and Prayer — 94

Unit 11
- Part 2•Section IIE-1, 3-5: Biblical Lifestyle: Distinctiveness/Humility; Integrity/Success; Simplicity/Greed — 95
- Part 2•Section IIE-2: Sexuality — 97
- Part 2•Section IIE-3: Power — 98
- Part 2•Section IIE-5: Generosity (Simplicity in Lifestyle) — 101

Unit 12
- Part 2•Section IIF-1: Unity and Partnership in Global Mission — 103
- Part 2•Section IIF-2: Partnership in Christian Mission — 105
- Part 2•Section IIF-3: Men and Women in Partnership — 108
- Part 2•Section IIF-4: Theological Education and Mission — 111

INTRODUCTION

The Cape Town Commitment, which issued from The Third Lausanne Congress of World Evangelization, in Cape Town, South Africa (16-25 October 2010), is in two parts. It opens with *The Cape Town Confession of Faith*, compiled by a team of theologians drawn globally, in preparation for The Third Lausanne Congress; and it is completed by *The Cape Town Call to Action*, which reflects the voices of leaders from 198 nations, gathered together in Cape Town, to work to discern what the Holy Spirit is saying to the church.

The following bibliography notes major sources relating to the Commitment's six themes. The listing, drawn together by a team of specialists, will, we trust, be useful for those building curricula in colleges and seminaries around the world. It is shaped to serve:

- courses on the text and context of *The Cape Town Commitment*
- classes on being a global Christian; and
- topical studies on areas of contemporary significance to mission.

The Third Lausanne Congress was based around six major themes: (i) Bearing witness to the truth of Christ in a pluralistic, globalized world; (ii) Building the peace of Christ in our divided and broken world; (iii) Living the love of Christ among people of other faiths; (iv) Discerning the will of Christ for world evangelization; (v) Calling the church of Christ back to humility, integrity and simplicity; (vi) Partnering in the body of Christ for unity in mission. Its program was developed as a result of unhurried consultation over a four-year period, with evangelical leaders on all continents. The *Commitment* is structured around these six themes.

As a suggestion for teaching, the following curriculum is broken down into 12 units, but may be used as flexibly as fits the class. NB the presence of a listed work is not an endorsement of all its contents; it is merely a recognition that the work relates in a distinctive way, and is worthy of consideration in an academic setting. Most titles recommended are from evangelical scholars. The resources are designed to give a solid orientation to the topic, and to lead into healthy discussion.

On topics where evangelicals have liberty to disagree, we have invited a range of contributions. The order of presentation is not reflective of ranking.

Structure

The designation reflects that of *The Cape Town Call Commitment*. In Part I (*The Cape Town Confession of Faith*) there are ten sections. In Part II (*The Cape Town Call to Action*), there are six major sections, broken down into subsections, denoted numerically. These are followed in some places by a further breakdown denoted by a letter. To distinguish the separate parts, the major sections in *The Cape Town Call to Action* are predicated with Part II in each case.

It is our prayer that this listing of works will encourage careful reflection and robust discussion; and that these, in turn, will lead to action, born out of passion for Christ. Students who follow this curriculum will be engaging the most vital topics of life: God's gospel, God's sovereign purposes, and God's saving and reconciling presence in our world.

Darrell Bock
Dallas Theological Seminary

Evvy Campbell
Wheaton College Graduate School

On behalf of the contributing team:

Contributor and Topic	Contributor and Topic
Mark Bailey - *Discipleship*	Anne-Christine Bataillard - *Children*
Judd Birdsall - *Religious Freedom*	Darrell Bock - *Our Love for the Gospel*
Gerry Breshears - *Men and Women in Partnership*	Peter Brierley - *Our Love for God's Mission*

Steve Bundy - *People with Disabilities*
Samuel Chiang - *Orality*
Sas Conradie - *Poverty, Simplicity, Generosity*
Lars Dahle - *Media*
Karl Dortzbach - *Ethnic Conflict*
Patrick Fung - *Unity*
John Franklin - *Arts*
Ken Gnanakan - *Truth and Pluralism*
Scott Horrell - *Our Love for God - Father, Son, Spirit*
Ravi Jayakaran - *Poverty*
Stan Jones - *Sexuality*
Tae Kang - *Our Love for God's People*
William Larkin - *Preamble, Our Love for God*
Celestin Masakura - *Suffering*
Todd Miles - *Truth and Pluralism*
Gregg Okesson - *Poverty, Distinctiveness, Integrity, Simplicity*
Mike Pocock - *Cities*
Ramesh Richard - *God's Love and Our Love*
Byron Spradlin - *Arts*
Lou Ann Stropoli - *Love and Other Faiths (all sections) Peoples*
Mats Tunehag - *Workplace*
Joseph Vijayam - *Workplace*
Tuvya Zaretsky - *Reconciliation and Jewish Evangelism*

M Daniel Carroll-Rodas - *Diaspora/Scattered Peoples*
Leiton Chinn - *Diaspora/Scattered Peoples*
Jane Crane - *Men and Women, and Power*
Debbie Dortzbach - *HIV/AIDS*
John Dyer - *Technology*
Dennis Fuqua - *Prayer*
Mitch Glaser - *Reconciliation and Jewish Evangelism*
David Horner - *Truth in Christ in a Pluralized World*
Chandler Im - *Diaspora/Scattered Peoples*
C. Nelson Jennings - *Our Love for the Word and the World*
Paul Joshua - *Leadership*
Manfred Kohl - *Public Institutions and Arenas*
Ben Lowe - *Stewardship and the Creation*
Doug McConnell - *Grace*
Matthew Niermann - *Arts*
Mark Overstreet - *Orality*
Greg Parsons - *Orality*
Karin Primuth - *Partnerships*
Rick Sessoms - *Leadership*
Steve Strauss - *Peace of Christ in a Globalized World*
Tim Tennent - *Theological Education and Mission*
Sadiri Joy Tira - *Diaspora/Scattered Peoples, Unreached*

Fernanda Vielma - *Humility*
Kristen Wiebe - *Slavery and Human Trafficking*

Recommended Class Texts

We recommend two books for all students:

The Cape Town Commitment Study Edition (Rose Dowsett. Peabody, Massachusetts: Hendrickson / Lausanne Library, 2012). This walks through the text with stimulating and searching questions on each section, suitable for use personally or in groups. Rose Dowsett, a UK missiologist with wide experience of tertiary-level teaching, was a member of the international Cape Town 2010 Statement Committee.

Christ our Reconciler (ed J.E.M. Cameron, Nottingham and Downers Grove, IVP / Lausanne Library, 2012). This substantial and pithy class reader, compiled from Congress addresses, sets the backdrop for *The Cape Town Commitment*. Each of the six major sections includes an exposition of Ephesians from a leading Bible teacher, and three or four presentations from some of the sharpest evangelical thinkers in their fields. The Foreword, by S. Douglas Birdsall, Executive Chairman of The Lausanne Movement, provides a summary explanation of both the context, and the goals, of the Congress.

For Bulk Copies

North America: The Lausanne bookstore, http://www.lausanne.christianbook.com

UK: The Lausanne bookstore, http://www.10ofThose.com/partners/lausanne

Africa, Asia, Latin America: Langham Literature, http://www.langhamcreative.org

Asia and the South Pacific: http://www.koorong.com, http://www.bookdepository.co.uk

Editor's Note

The Lausanne Movement uses British and American English. This curriculum was compiled in the US, so we have employed American spellings.

If a link does not work, please email documents@lausanne.org identifying the section.

If you have suggestions of further works to be added, email Julia Cameron, Lausanne Movement Director of Publishing (jcameron@lausanne.org). Kindly include a brief description of the contents with the usual formula of author and title, place and publisher. Where a book is published in more than one country, please list all publishers, as this curriculum will be used globally. We are grateful for your help in keeping this list up to date.

THE CAPE TOWN CONFESSION OF FAITH

UNIT I

PREAMBLE
The Historical Context of The Cape Town Commitment

John Stott. 'An Historical Introduction,' pp. xi-xxiv in John Stott (ed) *Making Christ Known: Historic Mission Documents from The Lausanne Movement 1974-1989* (Grand Rapids, Michigan: Eerdmans, 1996). These documents are also available at http://http://www.lausanne.org/en/documents/all.html

Charles E. Van Engen. 'Conciliar Mission Theology, 1930s -1990s,' pp. 145-56 in *Mission on the Way: Issues in Mission Theology* (Grand Rapids: Baker, 1996).

David J. Hesselgrave. 'Will We Correct the Edinburgh Error? Future Mission in Historical Perspective,' *Southwestern Journal of Theology* 49 (2007): pp. 121-49. Also available electronically through the ATLA database.

John Stott's preamble to *Making Christ Known* begins with a declaration of renewed commitment to the 'vision and goals of The Lausanne Movement.' In his 'Historical Introduction' he identifies the historical context of the Edinburgh World Missionary Conference (1910) and its aftermath, in which The Lausanne Movement arose under the seminal leadership of Billy Graham. He points to the 'poison of theological liberalism' which 'largely immobilized the churches' mission' (p. xii).

Charles E. Van Engen explains the theological constructs in conciliar mission theology, which promoted this immobilization: the redefinition of the relation of church and mission, in which a clear understanding of both was lost, and the re-conceptualization of mission as the church's socio-political usefulness for the world.

David Hesselgrave, on the eve of 2010 international mission conferences, including Cape Town 2010, calls for an avoidance of the error of Edinburgh (1910): mission strategy without prior doctrinal consensus. As an evangelical voice in harmony with The Lausanne Movement, Hesselgrave helps one understand why *The Cape Town Commitment* begins with a theological section: 'Our Confession of Faith.'

Lausanne I (Lausanne, Switzerland, 1974)

J. D. Douglas (ed). *Let the Earth Hear His Voice—International Congress on World Evangelization, Lausanne, Switzerland: Papers and Responses* (Minneapolis, Minnesota: World Wide Publications, 1975).

Lausanne Occasional Paper #3: John Stott. *The Lausanne Covenant: An Exposition and Commentary.* Available at http://www.lausanne.org/en/documents/lops/69-lop-3.html

Also available in the *Didasko Files* series (40pp) *The Lausanne Covenant: Complete text and study guide* (Peabody, Massachusetts: Hendrickson Publishers, 2012).

The preamble reminds us of the threefold fruit of Lausanne I: (i) *The Lausanne Covenant*; (ii) awareness of unreached people groups; (iii) a fresh discovery of the holistic nature of the biblical gospel and of Christian mission. Douglas' compendium provides essential background for understanding how these areas were developed. It includes Billy Graham's opening address, 'Why Lausanne?'

John Stott, chair of the drafting committee for *The Lausanne Covenant*, presents a very helpful exposition of its meaning, and of its place as the movement's foundational theological document. His address to the Congress on the process of drafting may be heard online at http://www2.wheaton.edu/bgc/archives/docs/Lausanne/704/stott.htm

Lausanne II (Manila, Philippines, 1989)

J. D. Douglas (ed). *Proclaim Christ Until He Comes: Calling the Whole Church to Take the Whole Gospel to the Whole Gospel to the Whole World* (Lausanne II in Manila, International Congress on World Evangelization, 1989, papers; Minneapolis, Minnesota: World Wide Publications, 1990).

Manila Manifesto Available at http://www.lausanne.org/en/documents/manila-manifesto.html

The preamble recognizes that The Lausanne Movement is committed to build on the work of the Second Lausanne Congress in Manila (1989). Douglas again edits an essential volume, *Proclaim Christ Until He Comes* (papers from Manila). *The Manila Manifesto*, present in Douglas, *Making Christ Known* (above), and online, stands in direct continuity with *The Lausanne Covenant* and captures in twenty-one affirmations, further expounded in twelve sections, its central doctrinal convictions and strategic mission commitments, fifteen years on.

The 'Unchanged Realities' section of the preamble to *The Manila Manfesto* articulates common themes expressed in the official documents and papers of both Lausanne I and Lausanne II.

The Third Lausanne Congress (Cape Town, South Africa 2010)

David Claydon (ed). *A New Vision, A New Heart, A Renewed Call: Lausanne Occasional Papers from 2004 Forum for World Evangelization hosted by Lausanne Committee for World Evangelization in Pattaya, Thailand, September 29- October 5, 2004* (Pasadena, CA: William Carey Library, 2005), 3 vols. Available as Lausanne Occasional Papers #30-60 at http://www.lausanne.org/en/documents/lops.html

Lausanne Theology Working Group, 2007-2010 Papers.
Available at http://www.lausanne.org/en/documents/all/twg/1234-twg-2007-2010.html

Lausanne Theology Working Group. 'The Whole Church taking the Whole Gospel to the Whole World: Reflections of the Lausanne Theology Working Group.'
Available at http://www.lausanne.org/en/documents/all/twg/1177-twg-three-wholes.html

'The Whole Church taking the Whole Gospel to the Whole World: Reflections of the Lausanne Theology Working Group'. With a summary of each theme.
http://www.lausanne.org/en/documents/cape-town-2010/1194-twg-three-wholes-condensed.html

Doug Birdsall, Address, Cape Town 2010 Opening Celebration. Available at
http://conversation.lausanne.org/en/conversations/detail/11322

Lindsay Brown, Closing Address, Cape Town 2010. Available at
http://conversation.lausanne.org/en/resources/detail/11646 [Also included (slightly shortened) in *Didasko Files* edition of *The Cape Town Commitment* (Peabody, Massachusetts: Hendrickson Publishers, 2011) and, in full, in J.E.M. Cameron (ed) *Christ our Reconciler: Gospel/Church/World* (Nottingham, UK and Downers Grove, Illinois IVP, 2012).]

The preamble shows how 'The Realities of Change', provide the context for the Third Lausanne Congress. The mission strategy portion of the Congress directly engaged these changing realities.

There were thirty-one Issue Groups in the preparatory Forum for World Evangelization (Pattaya, 2004). These provided the basis for global consultation on the framework and content for the programme, now represented in *The Cape Town Commitment* Part ll: *The Cape Town Call to Action*. David Claydon compiled papers from Pattaya (2004) in a comprehensive three volume collection. They are also available online as 'Lausanne Occasional Papers' (LOP #30-60). While written earlier, so without immediate past history, these complement well the plenary and multiplex addresses at Cape Town 2010.
(See *Cape Town 2010 Advance Papers* available at http://conversation.lausanne.org/en/advance_papers)

The preamble concludes with 'The Passion of Our Love', highlighting the three themes around which the Theology Working Group would conduct its discussions, namely the whole gospel, the whole world and the whole church.

In four consultations (2007-2010), the Theology Working Group, chaired by Chris Wright, explored each of these phrases in depth. 'The Whole Church taking the Whole Gospel to the Whole World: Reflections of the Lausanne Theology Working Group' combines the consultations' statements, and provides a summary of each theme.

Doug Birdsall's address at the Opening Celebration and Lindsay Brown's sermon at the Closing Ceremony capture many of the ideas of the preamble. The first prepares the delegates for the Congress' work; the second provides a concluding challenge to implement its theology, commitments, and mission strategy.

THE CAPE TOWN CONFESSION OF FAITH

UNIT 2

PART I • SECTION I
God's Love

Miroslav Volf. (November 2010). 'God is love: a basic Christian claim.' *Christian Century*, pp. 29-34. Article is available on ATLA Religion Database with ATLASerials. See also Miroslav Volf, 'God is Love: Biblical Reflections on a Fundamental Christian Claim in Conversation with Islam' (Chapter 5) in *Captive to the Word of God: Engaging the Scriptures for Contemporary Theological Reflection* (Grand Rapids, Michigan: Eerdmans, 2010).

In this brief and accessible article, Volf discusses the biblical nature of the doctrine that God is love, and explores how Christians may create an interfaith dialogue with Muslims on the topic. Instead of tiptoeing around controversial Christian claims, Volf seeks to discuss them openly, through Scripture, to help each group learn from the other. The article does not seek to blur the lines between the two religions; rather it aims to examine the misunderstandings Muslims have with Christian claims, to help better develop how the doctrines are presented to non-believers.

D. A. Carson. 'On Distorting the Love of God.' *Bibliotheca Sacra* 156 (1999); 3-12. Article is available on ATLA Religion Database with ATLASerials.

D. A. Carson. 'God is Love.' *Bibliotheca Sacra* 156 (1999): 131-142. Article is available on ATLA Religion Database with ATLASerials.

D. A. Carson. 'God's Love and God's Sovereignty.' *Bibliotheca Sacra* 156 (1999): 259-271. Article is available on ATLA Religion Database with ATLASerials.

D. A. Carson. 'God's Love and God's Wrath.' *Bibliotheca Sacra* 156 (1999): 387-398. Article is available on ATLA Religion Database with ATLASerials.

Carson seeks to show how the love of God is not as easy a doctrine as sometimes portrayed. The *first* article discusses how the popularity of this doctrine has caused it to become oversimplified and then shows the necessary diversity of God's love seen in Scripture. The *second* article explores the many different aspects of the Father's love for the Son found in John 5:16-30, ending with a brief discussion of how this relates to humanity. The *third* article speaks to God's love of humanity as mediated through his sovereignty, seeking to explain why the two attributes cannot be divorced from one another. In the *final* article, Carson writes about how the wrath of God and the love of God are not mutually exclusive, examining it through the atonement, God's love for the world, and God's love for his people. Portions of this series leave the strict realm of God's love, and briefly discuss our love flowing from the Father's love. These sections, while not lengthy, open the doors to a more informed discussion of what it means for our love to imitate God's love.

Thomas H. McCall. *Forsaken: The Trinity, the Cross and Why it Matters* (Downers Grove, Illinois: IVP Academic, 2012).

McCall approaches one of the most disconcerting moments in Jesus' life from a Trinitarian view, his cry to God asking why he has been forsaken; this helps us understand what is happening in that moment. Chapter 2 ('Did the Death of Jesus Make it Possible for God to Love Me?') is the most pertinent to the discussion of God's love for us, but the whole book helps one gain a deeper appreciation of how much God loves us. By looking at (a) what occurred in the Trinity at that moment, (b) the purpose of the crucifixion, and (c) what it means to us, one sees what great lengths God went to in saving his creation and how his love was manifested.

Werner G. Jeanrond. *A Theology of Love* (London: T&T Clark, 2010).

Jeanrond explores the biblical sentiments on love, and how love is treated in literature and culture. He sifts through different approaches to Christian love as presented in theology and considers the biblical foundations undergirding each. There is a thought-provoking exploration of the differences between God's love for us, our love for God, and our love for one another. The final chapter looks at the love of God in regard to topics such as creation, salvation, forgiveness, and sexuality (a topic which is often not analyzed).

Lewis Sperry Chafer. *True Evangelism: Winning Souls Through Prayer* (Grand Rapids: Kregel, 1993 [1919]).

Chafer's short piece, a classic in the field of evangelism, deals effectively with the subject of God's love and our love. Chafer first works through God's love for humanity, poured out through Christ's death on the cross. Then he shows how the believer's love will change to mimic God's love as he grows in communion with God.

Craig Ott, Stephen J. Strauss with Timothy C. Tennent. 'Part 1 Biblical Foundations of Mission' (Chapters 1-6) in *Encountering Theology of Mission: Biblical Foundations, Historical Developments, and Contemporary Issues* (Grand Rapids: Baker Academic, 2010).

These six chapters lay out a working theology of God's love as seen in the realm of missions. The book begins by exploring what the Old and New Testaments say about missions (specifically God's heart towards people) and then moves into how believers are to bring a continuing presence of God's love.

James I. Packer. 'The Love of God: Universal and Particular' (Chapter 11) in *Celebrating the Saving Work of God: Collected Shorter Writings of J.I. Packer* (Paternoster Press, 1998). This writing is also available in Thomas R. Schriener and Bruce A. Ware, *The Grace of God, the Bondage of Will* (Grand Rapids: Baker Book House, 1995).

The usefulness of this article is in the breadth of ways it discusses how God's love is seen or experienced. It challenges readers to examine their usage of the word 'love' and to compare it with the Ultimate Love. It speaks not only of how the Bible portrays God's love, but of how different theological methods portray it. The author states his position, while giving a fair view of others' readings.

Brennan Manning. 'Embracing Ourselves with God's Love in Our Brokenness (Original Title Unavailable)' Staley Lectures (Seattle: Seattle Pacific University, 1996). This title is available for free on iTunes University from Seattle Pacific University.

Manning pours over memories of anguish which pushed him to realize that he believed God loved him only when he could love himself. He challenges the listener to join with Christ in loving the broken; and the broken are not only outsiders but also ourselves as we find ourselves broken. He claims that often we feel the love of God only when we judge ourselves to be worthy of it; it becomes something we earn. He shows that God's love transcends our shortcomings, and is greater than the failings we have inside ourselves.

A. W. Tozer. *God's Pursuit of Man* (Camp Hill, Pennsylvania: WingSpread, 2007). Also published under the titles *The Divine Conquest* and *The Pursuit of Man*. See also A. W. Tozer, *The Pursuit of God* (Camp Hill, Pennsylvania: WingSpread, 2006).

This book, which looks at God's love for humanity, is a companion to Tozer's more known work *The Pursuit of God* (where he looks at how a person can grow in love for God). Tozer shows that, from the very beginning, God had a plan to save creation. He explores characteristics of God, such as jealousy, and how each reveals more of God's love to us. Ultimately, this book aims to show the reader that God is the one who is always seeking after man, and not the other way around.

James Philip. *The Glory of the Cross: The great crescendo of the gospel* (*Didasko Files* series. Peabody, Massachusetts: Hendrickson / Lausanne Library, 2012).

This 32pp *Didasko File* walks through the gospel narrative from the Last Supper to Calvary, expounding Christ's 'fierce, costly love'. James Philip's profound and perceptive grasp of the gospel reveals rich new insights, in an unusual blend of doctrinal truth and pastoral application. Its short length belies its depth. Includes questions for reflection. Foreword by Sinclair B. Ferguson.

THE CAPE TOWN CONFESSION OF FAITH

UNIT 3

PART I • SECTION 2
Our Love for God

John Piper. *Desiring God: Meditations of a Christian Hedonist* (Portland, Oregon: Multnomah, 1986; Nottingham, UK: IVP Updated Edition, 2004). Available for free at http://www.desiringgod.org/resource-library/online-books/desiring-god

Boyd Luter. (March 1988). "'Worship' as service: the New Testament usage of latreuō.' *Criswell Theological Review* 4 (1988): pp. 335-344. Article is available on ATLA Religion Database with ATLASerials.

Vaughan Roberts. *True Worship* (Authentic Media, 2002).

All three writers look at worship as a way of life. Piper's book *Desiring God* looks at the theology from the perspective that when God is our everything, he is most pleased with us. In essence, by loving God we bring him joy. So even our love for him can be an act of service. As Piper works through different passages of Scripture, he encourages the reader to begin living a life where worshiping God is one's sole purpose. A person should not only live for this, but also find joy in it.

Luter works through a small number of New Testament passages examining how the word for worship is used in each. He argues that while the worship service is important, our lives should express worship outside of what happens on Sunday.

Vaughan Roberts, a pastor in Oxford, UK, and a Cape Town 2010 expositor, opens with the foundation of Christian worship 'in spirit and in truth'. He deals with the nature of truth, and its outworking, concluding with the meaning of the Lord's Supper.

Scot McKnight. 'The *Jesus Creed*: A spiritually formed person loves God by following Jesus, and loves others.' (Chapters 1-6) and 'Living the *Jesus Creed*: A spiritually formed person loves Jesus' (Chapters 19-24) in *The Jesus Creed: Loving God, Loving Others* (Brewster, MA: Paraclete Press, 2004).

Mark Allan Powell. *Loving Jesus* (Minneapolis: Fortress Press, 2004).

Both titles present a case that spiritual formation begins and ends with loving God.

McKnight approaches the topic of loving God from the perspective of spiritual formation; if a person wants to grow, then he or she must begin with their love for God. His focus throughout the work is that if the *Shema* was the center of Judaism, then when Jesus quotes the *Shema*, adding Leviticus 19:18, this teaching should be at the heart of our Christian walk. Powell argues that when people want to become spiritual, they are looking for change within. The greatest change that can occur within a human is to love God first and foremost. Throughout his book he tackles the issue of loving God, and how we can express our love for God.

Mark Allan Powell. 'Part One: Belonging to God' (Chapters 1-3) in *Giving to God: The Bible's Good News about Living a Generous Life* (Grand Rapids, Michigan: Eerdmans, 2006).

Powell's book looks at the act of giving as a tangible expression of loving God. He explores the realm of finding joy in giving from what God has given to us. This is very different from a sense of stewardship borne out of duty. He also explores giving as a spiritual discipline, to allow us to find true satisfaction in God as we grow closer to him.

Ramesh Richard. *Soul Passion: Embracing Your Life's Ultimate Purpose* (Chicago: Moody Publishers, 2003). See also Ramesh Richard, *Soul Mission* and *Soul Vision* (Chicago: Moody Publishers, 2004).

David K. Naugle. *Reordered Love, Reordered Lives: Learning The Deep Meaning of Happiness* (Grand Rapids, Michigan: Eerdmans, 2008).

These two works look at the practical side of our love for God, seeking to re-orient the believer's passion for him. Richard's work fuses love with passion and purpose, as it explores the way we actually live, and compares it with the way God has called us to live. By approaching life in this way, we see the man-made ways we encourage ourselves to live, as opposed to the biblical ways. Richard makes the discussion practical by leading us to look at our own lives.

Naugle looks at man's love for God by coupling it with happiness, and exploring man's ways to seek happiness through lesser creations. He exposes our cravings through studying how man instinctively orients his life. He also brings to light the many failings in a life void of love for God, which include not knowing how to love self or others. Finally, he looks at how we could reorder our lives to love God better, individually and as a body.

Matthew A. Elliott. 'Love,' pp. 135-164 in his *Faithful Feelings: Rethinking Emotion in the New Testament* (Grand Rapids, Michigan: Kregel, 2006).

Elliot works to overturn the common Christian belief that love is a duty, by showing that in the New Testament it is also viewed as a feeling. The author examines both current and classical theologians' writings on the topic and looks at the Greek usage of words translated as love. From here, he re-examines passages in the New Testament to see if they speak of an emotional side of love. The author straddles a fine line throughout the section as he deals with practically-expressed love and ethereal love, noting that both are to be present in the discussion.

Christopher J. H. Wright. *The Mission of God: Unlocking the Bible's Grand Narrative* (Downers Grove, Illinois: IVP, 2006): Chapters 3-4, 'The Living God Makes Himself Known in Israel'; 'The Living God Makes Himself Known in Jesus Christ.'

Chris Wright expounds the Old and New Testament evidence for the Triune God as 'Creator, Ruler, Judge and Savior' in several chapters of this seminal work.

Christopher J. H. Wright. *The Mission of God: Unlocking the Bible's Grand Narrative* (Downers Grove, Illinois: IVP, 2006): Chapter 5, 'The Living God Confronts Idolatry.'

Scott Moreau. 'Contextualization, Syncretism, and Spiritual Warfare: Identifying the Issues,' pp. 47-70 in Gailyn Van Rheenen (ed). *Contextualization and Syncretism: Navigating the Cultural Currents* (EMS Ser. 13; Pasadena, CA: William Carey Library, 2006).

Wayne Grudem. *Politics-According the Bible: A Comprehensive Resource for Understanding Modern Political Issues in Light of Scripture* (Grand Rapids: Zondervan, 2010).

LOP #31: 'The Uniqueness of Christ in a Postmodern World and the Challenge of World Religions.' Available at http://www.lausanne.org/en/documents/lops/844-lop-31.html

Christopher J. H. Wright. 'Calling the Church Back to Humility, Integrity and Simplicity' (Cape Town 2010 Advance Paper). Available at http://conversation.lausanne.org/en/conversations/detail/10520
See also Cape Town 2010 Congress video, 'Integrity – Confronting Idols.' Available at http://conversation.lausanne.org/en/conversations/detail/11556

Chris Wright provides background for this *CTC* paragraph in his thorough discussion of the biblical teaching on the nature of gods and idols vis-à-vis the one true God. He presents a biblically-informed missional approach to idolatry in all its variety. He also treats its deleterious effects. He calls for a confrontation with idolatry which will involve 'theological argument, evangelistic engagement, pastoral guidance, and prophetic warning.'

Addressing the same *CTC* topics concerning idolatry in our day, Moreau clearly defines 'syncretism' and describes its presence in various dimensions of religion using Ninian Smart's taxonomy. He also provides a four-step approach to combating syncretism.

Wayne Grudem provides an example of 'a biblical critique of political ideology.'

LOP #31: 'The Uniqueness of Christ in a Postmodern World and the Challenge of World Religions' not only expounds the biblical and theological foundations for the 'uniqueness of Christ,' but discusses methods for communicating it in the context of religious pluralism. The report looks at how the doctrine relates to 'traces of Jesus in non-Christian religions'.

Chris Wright in both his Cape Town 2010 Advance Paper and Congress Address develops the areas in which the church needs to be called to repent: from the idolatry of power to the call to humility; the idolatry of success to the call to integrity; the idolatry of greed to the call to simplicity.

John Piper. *Let the Nations be Glad! The Supremacy of God in Missions* (3rd ed Grand Rapids: Baker, 2010): Chapter 1, 'The Supremacy of God in Missions through Worship.'

John Stott. *The Message of Romans: God's Good News for the World* (BST; Downers Grove, Illinois: IVP, 2001).

John C. Lennox. *Gunning for God: Why the New Atheists Are Missing the Target* (Grand Rapids: Kregel, 2011).

Edward Rommen and Harold Netland (eds). *Christianity and the Religions: A Biblical Theology of World Religions* (EMS Ser. 2; Pasadena, CA: William Carey Library, 1995).

Darrell L. Bock and Daniel B. Wallace. *Dethroning Jesus: Exposing Popular Culture's Quest to Unseat the Biblical Christ* (Nashville, TN: Thomas Nelson, 2007).

LOP #10: 'Christian Witness to Nominal Christians Among Roman Catholics.' Available at
http://www.lausanne.org/en/documents/lops/55-lop-10.html

LOP #19: 'Christian Witness to Nominal Christians Among the Orthodox.' Available at
http://www.lausanne.org/en/documents/lops/64-lop-19.html

LOP #23: 'Christian Witness to Nominal Christians Among Protestants.' Available at
http://www.lausanne.org/en/documents/lops/66-lop-23.html

John Piper's now famous assertion, 'Missions is not the ultimate goal of the church. Worship is. Missions exists because worship doesn't' (*Let the Nations be Glad!* p. 11) opens a chapter, which articulates the theme of this CTC paragraph: worship, bringing glory to God is the greatest motivation for missions. In support of this theme, John Stott is quoted extensively from his exposition of the phrase 'for the sake of his name' in Romans 1:5. Stott labels this the sixth 'fundamental truth' about the gospel from Romans 1:1-6, namely, 'the goal of the gospel is the honour of Christ's name.'

John Lennox, Oxford mathematician and apologist, deals with the main contentions of 'aggressive atheism': God and science are incompatible; religion is deleterious; the biblical God is a despot; the atonement is morally repugnant.

Rommen and Netland contains a comprehensive biblical theology of religions from all sections of the Old and New Testament as a framework for viewing 'world religions.'

Bock and Wallace answer six key claims in current North American 'popular culture' which 'abuse and misrepresent Jesus,' including (i) Jesus' message was primarily political; (ii) the Gnostic gospels, such as the Gospel of Judas and the Gospel of Thomas, radically alter our understanding of Jesus; and (iii) Paul with his exaltation of Christ and inclusion of the Gentiles altered the original Jewish reform movement of Jesus and James.

From the Lausanne archives of Lausanne Occasional Papers come three reports of mini-consultations on 'Christian Nominalism' (among Roman Catholics, the Orthodox, and Protestants) at 1980 Pattaya COWE. Each report addresses the issues of defining; the current situation of the group; and a strategy for reaching nominals in the group.

Michael Herbst. 'Witnessing to Christ in a Secular Culture' (Cape Town 2010 Advance Paper). Available at
http://conversation.lausanne.org/en/conversations/detail/10580
See also Cape Town 2010 Congress video, 'Truth - Presenting Truth in Europe.' Available at
http://conversation.lausanne.org/en/conversations/detail/11390

Os Guinness. 'Why Truth Matters' See Cape Town 2010 Congress video, 'Truth – Why Truth Matters.' Available at http://conversation.lausanne.org/en/conversations/detail/11392
See also Cape Town 2010 Session Summary and Segment Synopsis, 'TRUTH: Making the Case for the Truth of Christ in a Puralistic, Globalized World.' Available at http://www.lausanne.org/docs/capetown2010/summaries/P218-Truth.pdf

Also in J.E.M. Cameron (ed) Christ our Reconciler (Nottingham and Downers Grove: IVP, 2012).

LOP #42: 'Prayer in Evangelism.' Available at http://www.lausanne.org/en/documents/lops/857-lop-42.html

Christopher R. Little. *Mission in the Way of Paul: Biblical Mission for the Church in the Twenty-first Century* (New York: Peter Lang, 2005): Chapter 3, 'The Theological and Practical Orientation of Pauline Mission.'

CTC explains the character of the witness to which we are called to commit ourselves, as modeled in the Congress addresses of Herbst and Guinness, together with the report of Issue Group No. 13 'Prayer in Evangelism' from the Forum for World Evangelization, Pattaya 2004.

Michael Herbst is an evangelist to a skeptical, dismissive post-socialist Europe, particularly the former GDR. Herbst describes how a 'bold but humble witness to our God' must come as Jesus did in the Incarnation: 'still *the* word, but he became 'flesh'—a universal truth claim in a very humble presentation.' Yes, there will be firm conviction about the exclusiveness of Christ's truth claim, and a confidence born of dependence on the Holy Spirit to work. But this bold witness will be a humble witness to Christ 'from below', in loving service which wins trust.

Os Guinness, British apologist, in his Congress address, 'Why Truth Matters' embodied a 'robust and gracious defense of the truth of the gospel of Christ.' He presented six reasons why truth matters:
- it is theological, about God;
- it is absolute and exclusive in Christ—the only way to God;
- it empowers our best human enterprises in all spheres of life;
- it undergirds proclamation and defense of the faith;
- only it is sufficient to combat evil and hypocrisy;
- it nurtures growth and transformation in Christ.

The report from the Pattaya 2004 'Prayer in Evangelism' issue group calls for a witness characterized by a 'prayerful trust in the convicting and convincing work of God's Holy Spirit.' It also presents a theology and motivation, together with principles and guidelines, for prayer in evangelism. It considers such allied topics as spiritual warfare, healing, fasting, children and strategies. And it concludes with practical suggestions for spiritually-healthy praying related to world evangelism in a 'Life Prayer Plan for World Evangelism.'

The 'Commitment to Witness' climaxes with a forceful declaration of the goal, and hence the motivation, for the witness of those who love God. This involves a sharing of 'God's greatest priority, which is that his name and his Word should be exalted above all things.'

Little develops this doxological aim of mission both in its presence across the entire sweep of Scripture and Paul's articulation and implementation of it in the church and in society.

THE CAPE TOWN CONFESSION OF FAITH

UNIT 4

PART I • SECTIONS 3-5
God as Father, Son and Spirit: The Trinity

The works below focus on why we are called to love the Father, the Son, and the Holy Spirit. A fourth bibliography on God as Holy Trinity unifies these sections and provides essential teaching to deepen our understanding of each Person as well as of the Godhead as a whole. The Trinitarian bibliography (see below the separate sections) will act as the framework for these three sections.

PART I • SECTION 3
The Father

Few books in recent decades have focused on the Person of God the Father, 'the forgotten member of the Godhead' (Gerald Bray). This is likely an over-reaction to 19th and early 20th century liberalism's theme of 'the Fatherhood of God and the brotherhood of man' which denied the deity of Jesus Christ and the distinction of the Spirit. Most works on 'God' and the divine attributes presume that the Father is especially in view, but not many address the Person of God the Father.

J. S. Lidgett. *The Fatherhood of God.* Edited version, Minneapolis: Bethany, 1987; 1st ed (Edinburgh: 1902).

Noted Anglican churchman and educator, Lidgett (1854–1953) presents an overview of God the Father in both New and Old Testaments, beginning with Jesus' teaching. He then traces the theological development of the Father God through church history, with applications in both doctrine and practice. Written at the culmination of nineteenth-century liberalism when divine fatherhood overshadowed any deity of Christ and the Spirit, Lidgett's work remains a classic: balanced, scholarly, orthodox, and devotional.

Alan P. F. Sell. *God Our Father: Doctrine and Devotion.* Rev. ed, Shippensburg Pennsylvania: Ragged Edge, 2000; 1st ed (Edinburgh: The Saint Andrew Press).

Former theological secretary of the World Alliance of Reformed Churches and professor of theology in Canada and Wales, Sell leads readers through traditional doctrinal and devotional literature to engender love for God the Father. While almost exclusively North Atlantic in its orientation, the applications are easily universal.

Christopher J. H. Wright. *Knowing God the Father Through the Old Testament* (Downers Grove Illinois: IVP, 2007).

Written with depth and devotion, Chris Wright's work completes his trilogy on Knowing Jesus, Knowing the Spirit, and Knowing the Father from the Old Testament. What do we mean when we pray 'Our Father in heaven'? (a title foreign to, yet grounded in, the Old Testament). Chapter titles outline the book's contents: Knowing God as a Father in Action, Through Experience of His Grace, Through Exposure to Judgment, as the Father of His People, Through Engaging Him in Prayer, Through Reflecting His Justice, Through Returning His Love, in Expectation of His Victory, and Through Trusting His Sovereignty.

Marianne Meye Thompson. *The Promise of the Father: Jesus and God in the New Testament* (Louisville Kentucky: Westminster John Knox, 2000).

For theologically-informed readers, Thompson's book looks at the meaning of speaking of God as Father, Abba, particularly through the lens of Jesus' relation to and teaching about the Father in the gospels. Discerning readers will also sense feminist concerns that God not be conceived as gendered, and that the masculine language for God not affirm the patriarchal hierarchy of historic Christendom.

http://www.theopedia.com/God_the_Father

http://www.arielm.org/dcs/pdf/mbs051m.pdf

> The Theopedia site entails a precise summation of the historical doctrine of God the Father (2pp). God is the *principium* of divinity, thus often termed 'the First Person' of the Trinity, without denying the co-eternality and equality of each Person as fully God.
>
> *God the Father* Ariel Ministries booklet by Arnold Fruchtenbaum (pdf. 2005, 7pp). A biblical study—accurate, compact, and readable, from a Messianic Jewish perspective.
>
> Both readings are without charge and highly recommended.

Timothy George. *Is the Father of Jesus the God of Muhammad?* (Grand Rapids: Zondervan, 2002).

Miroslav Volf. *Allah: A Christian Response* (New York: HarperOne, 2011).

> In the midst of tensions between Islam and the Christian faith, the authors compare the similarities and differences in the concepts of God, and neither provides simplistic answers. Written in the wake of destruction of the Twin Towers in New York City (2001), George's work concludes that God the Father of Jesus is also the God whom Paul proclaimed to Athenian philosophers on Mars Hill; that is, there is a place for a universal appeal to the high God of theism.
>
> Written a decade later, Volf's more sophisticated work attempts to bridge the divide with Islam, stressing unifying themes between the Allah of earlier Arabic Christian faith and the Allah of Islam. He encourages interfaith dialogue, global peace, and co-habitation with Islam.
>
> Volf and George—both known for their Trinitarian writings—explain and defend the central Christian understanding of God as Father, Son, and Holy Spirit.

PART I • SECTION 4
The Son

Christopher J. H. Wright. *Knowing Jesus Through the Old Testament* (Downers Grove Illinois: IVP, 1995).

Chris Wright pastorally articulates Jesus' self-identity as rooted in the history of Israel. This book, which led to a Trinitarian exploration of the Hebrew Scriptures, unfolds the Savior's relation to the Old Testament's story, promise, Messianic identity, mission, and values. For Wright, God's design for Israel is fulfilled in Jesus Christ.

Richard Bauckham. *Jesus and the God of Israel* (Grand Rapids, Michigan: Eerdmans, 2008).

Bauckham, Senior Scholar at Ridley Hall, Cambridge, argues for a growing conviction of the deity of Christ early in the NT church. Of special note is Chapter 1 'God Crucified,' a revised edition of his 1998 publication. He then clarifies other evidences for Jesus' divinity from Mark, the Pauline epistles, Hebrews, all within the Jewish understanding of God in the first century. Chapters serve well for discussion points on a graduate level.

Darrell L. Bock. *Jesus According to Scripture: Restoring the Portrait from the Gospels* (Grand Rapids: Baker, 2002).

The value of this sizeable volume in a study of *The Cape Town Commitment* is that Bock integrates the multiple gospel themes and portraits of the Savior. *Jesus According to Scripture* gathers each of the gospel writers' accounts into cohesive units, to help elucidate their different perspectives. The work concludes with a theological portrait of Jesus.

Robert M. Bowman, Jr. and J. Ed Komoszewski. *Putting Jesus in His Place: The Case for the Deity of Christ* (Grand Rapids: Kregel, 2007).

Here is an exciting, widely-acclaimed defense that Jesus is God because he shares the honors, attributes, names, activities, and finally the very throne of God the Father. Easy to read, rich in content, designed for broad readership and study, the book evokes our love for Him Who Is Worthy and gives confidence in making him known.

Josh McDowell and Sean McDowell. *More Than a Carpenter.* Revised edition. (Wheaton Illinois: Tyndale House/Living Books, 2009).

McDowell freshens his case for the deity of Jesus Christ. Earlier editions are available in at least 85 languages and continue to challenge non-Christians to faith in Christ, and to equip believers to better proclaim him as the Son of God. A pdf download of the introduction is available at http://www.tyndale.com/More-Than-a-Carpenter/9781414326276

John Piper. *What Jesus Demands from the World.* Reprint. (Wheaton Illinois: Crossway, 2011).

Piper, respected pastor and author, insists that if we love Christ, we will obey him. Jesus' reveals who he is and what he expects of us through his demands of allegiance in the gospels. Jesus' commands, far from selfish control, lead us to the believer's good, satisfaction, and love for our Lord and God the Father. Slices of the book provide rich discussion. Note also the Desiring God website with multiple articles and sermons. http://www.desiringgod.org/resource-library/articles/by-topic

Scot McKnight. 'The Jesus We'll Never Know.' *Christianity Today*, April 2010, 22-26. And 'Should We Abandon Studying the Historical Jesus? Two Responses,' by N. T. Wright and Craig Keener, pp. 27-28.

Useful as a discussion starter. McKnight, an evangelical, argues that Jesus scholars construct a kind of fifth gospel that never quite matches the canonical Jesus. His posture of skepticism toward reconstructions of the historical Jesus is disputed by two other New Testament scholars, N. T. Wright and Craig Keener— who both affirm the propriety of historical studies with reasoned defense. This defense is also available online at the *Christianity Today* web site with an additional response by Darrell Bock at http://www.christianitytoday.com/ct/2010/aprilweb-only/24-51.0.html

Collin Hansen. 'The Son and the Crescent.' *Christianity Today*, February 2011, pp. 18–23.

Hansen discusses current tensions regarding the translation of 'Son of God' in Muslim idiom Bible translations. Translation issues involve much more than a regard for the Islamic context (where such a phrase is deemed blasphemous). Hansen's focus here is on the polarization among Christians because of non-literal renderings for 'Son of God' and other familiar terms for God (*eg* 'Father').

http://bible.org/seriespage/christology-jesus-christ#TopOfPage

http://www.desiringgod.org/resource-library/articles/how-can-jesus-be-god-and-man

Among many reliable works at Bible.org and DesiringGod.org, two biblical overviews highlight different aspects of Christology. Greg Herrick (2004) provides a holistic synopsis of the doctrine of Christ (6pp). Matt Perman provides a condensed review (6pp) of the two natures—divine and human—in the one Person of Jesus Christ. Both articles sustain the Definition of Chalcedon in AD 451. Many students of theology as well as broader readership find such primers helpful.

http://www.thespurgeonfellowship.org/Downloads/feature_Sp08.pdf by D.A. Carson.

Here D.A. Carson sets out to define the Gospel as Jesus Christ himself. Many have tried to redefine it in terms that actually negate who Jesus Christ is and what he accomplished through his death and resurrection. Dr. Carson shows that such efforts are fallacious and completely inadequate to explain much of Scripture not the least 1 Corinthians 15. The Gospel of Jesus Christ compels our belief in him, our obedience to him, and our proclamation of him. Carson sets out these and more in this lengthy, informative piece on the Gospel and Person of Jesus Christ.

http://bible.org/seriespage/christology-jesus-christ#TopOfPage by Dr. Greg Herrick.

In this article the author presents an overview of Christology. This serves as a good primer for who Christ is, what he has done; and why we should believe in the historical orthodox tenets believed and passed onto us.

Part I • Section 5
The Holy Spirit

Christopher J. H. Wright. *Knowing the Holy Spirit Through the Old Testament* (Downers Grove Illinois: IVP, 2006).

This is a series of lectures for students desiring to understand the working of the Spirit of Yahweh in the OT, further revealed in the NT. The following are also valuable in their treatments of the Spirit. The titles make their contents clear:

Gordon Fee. *Paul, the Spirit, and the People of God* (Peabody MA: Hendrickson, 1996).

Fee is Professor Emeritus at Regent College, Vancouver BC. Here we have various gems from his massive *God's Empowering Presence: The Holy Spirit in the Letters of Paul* (Peabody MA: Henderickson, 1994). This is a delightfully readable work available in several languages. Fee presents a doctrine of the Spirit and the Spirit's work in the church that is firmly grounded in the New Testament. His approach is for all evangelicals, and much of what he writes is directly relevant to the Spirit's power in evangelism and mission.

Graham A. Cole. *He Who Gives Life: The Doctrine of the Holy Spirit* (Wheaton Illinois: Crossway, 2007).

One of the best theologies of the Spirit is that of former principal of Ridley College, University of Melbourne, now at Trinity Evangelical Divinity School. Beginning with 'The Mystery of the Spirit', Cole acquaints us with the Person of the Spirit through the Spirit's ministries in Old and New Testaments. He addresses a host of practical problems (eg may we pray to the Spirit?). Cole appreciates that the Spirit reflects the selflessness of the Triune God.

Craig S. Keener. *The Spirit in the Gospels and Acts: Divine Purity and Power* (Peabody MA: Hendrickson, 1997).

Keener's more academic work is a popularization of his Duke University doctoral dissertation. He complements Wright's work in the Old Testament and Fee's in Pauline literature. After background studies of the Spirit in inter-testamental Judaism, Keener highlights Jesus' role as 'the Spirit-Bringer' in Mark and Matthew; the Spirit's place in John's Gospel; and Luke's portrayal of the Spirit culminating in the pouring forth at Pentecost.

Francis Chan. *Forgotten God: Reversing Our Tragic Neglect of the Holy Spirit*. New ed (Colorado Springs Colorado: David C. Cook, 2009).

Chan, a popular speaker, and pastor of Cornerstone Church in Simi Valley, California, aims beyond issues that divide evangelicals and Pentecostals, to address matters which help all readers to love and to trust the Holy Spirit in daily life. His humble attitude and practical approach has contagious appeal.

Amos Yong. *The Spirit Poured Out on All Flesh: Pentecostalism and the Possibility of Global Theology.* (Grand Rapids: Baker, 2005).

Yong, a Pentecostal born in Malaysia, and a prolific scholar at Regent University (Virginia Beach, Virginia), discusses the Person and work of the Spirit, and explores much more. His passion is to expand our understanding of the Spirit's activity in the world, in relation to broader ecumenism or even to non-Christian religions. Yong's work challenges evangelical categories.

J. L. Story. 'Pauline Thoughts about the Holy Spirit and Sanctification: Provision, Process, and Consummation.' *Journal of Pentecostal Theology* 18: 1 (2009): pp. 67-94.

Story examines Pauline texts to show that sanctification through the Holy Spirit involves (i) God's provision in his gracious call, (ii) the process of sanctification in Christian growth in moral purity and love, and (iii) the consummation at the *parousia*. The author argues for the comprehensive role of the Spirit in the past event, present experience, and future hope of the people of God, and argues for a consistency between the three activities, always including the essential element of love.

Veli-Matti Kärkkäinen. *Pneumatology: The Holy Spirit in Ecumenical, International, and Contextual Perspective* (Grand Rapids: Baker, 2002).

http://bible.org/seriespage/survey-bible-doctrine-holy-spirit by Sid Litke

This is a great overview of Pneumatology. While we don't have to know everything about God the Holy Spirit in order to love him and all he has done in our lives as well as what He is doing in the world, such an article is very beneficial because it provides the biblical framework within which one ought to think about the third Person of the Trinity.

http://bible.org/seriespage/spirit-and-community-historical-perspective

Here is a brief historical survey of the perceived role of the Holy Spirit within the Christian community. Many mistakes have been made throughout the history of the Church. Will we learn from them or repeat them?

http://bible.org/seriespage/spirit-and-community-historical-perspective by Gerald Bray

Gerald Bray, the well-known Anglican professor at Beeson Divinity School, Birmingham Alabama, writes 'The Spirit and Community: A Historial Perspective' (9pp). He evaluates how 'the Spirit-led community' has been understood at different times from the medieval church until today. Protestant theology developed a doctrine of the invisible church, yet the invisible church is manifest in a multitude of ways. In his desire to explore new ways to build Spirit-led communities, Bray concludes with a challenge to evangelicals to re-examine basic assumptions.

http://en.wikipedia.org/wiki/Holy_Spirit

Greg Herrick's 'Pneumatology: The Holy Spirit' (4pp) provides a simple biblical framework to think about the 3rd Person of the Trinity. We commend this article on 'Holy Spirit' contrasting the Christian understanding of the Spirit with that of Judaism, Islam, and Baha'i (2pp). We acknowledge that an article on Wikipedia, by its nature, may not remain as originally authored, and readers should be mindful of this.

Part I • Sections 3-5
The Trinity

Thomas Oden (ed). *Ancient Christian Doctrine*, 5 vols. (Downers Grove Illinois: IVP, 2009-2010).

Thomas Oden. *Classical Christianity: A Systematic Theology* (New York: HarperOne, 2009).

The earliest creeds are built around the Matthean baptismal formula, 'in the name of the Father, and of the Son and of the Holy Spirit' (28:19). Significant scholarly research is being done in the patristic fathers' writings regarding the Trinity. Highly recommended for all seminary libraries is the 5-volume series *Ancient Christian Doctrine* (ACD, above) which draws together thousands of patristic quotations around the Nicene-Constantinopolitan Creed (AD 325/381). The ACD series is richly complemented by Oden's *Classical Christianity: A Systematic Theology* (New York: HarperOne, 2009) 916pp, structured around the three Persons and activities of the Trinity.

Two new collections of essays inform every side of biblical, historical and contemporary Trinitarianism, including global and interfaith dialogue. The larger first volume is more holistic, especially regarding Trinity in dogmatics and Christian praxis. The latter *Cambridge Companion* addresses contemporary Trinitarianism and interfaith dialogue. Highly commended.

Gilles Emory and Matthew Levering (eds). *The Oxford Handbook of the Trinity* (Oxford UK: Oxford University Press, 2011).

Peter C. Phan (ed). *The Cambridge Companion to the Trinity* (Cambridge UK: Cambridge University Press, 2011).

In addition several more works on the Trinity are recommended for diverse emphases:

Robert Letham. *The Holy Trinity: In Scripture, History, Theology, and Worship* (Phillipsburg, New Jersey: P&R, 2004).

Letham, Systematic theologian at the Wales Evangelical School of Theology, has written the premier single volume on the doctrine of the Trinity. Reformed and conservative, his highly-regarded theology is comprehensive, astute in historical and contemporary Trinitarian assessment, and worshipful in its exaltation of the Triune God.

Fred Sanders. *The Deep Things of God: How the Trinity Changes Everything* (Wheaton Illinois: Crossway, 2010).

Sanders, of Biola University's Torrey Honors Institute, enjoyably recounts the long experiential history of evangelicals and Trinitarian faith. He offers rich insights as to how biblical salvation and mission are directly related to the activity of the Father, Son, and Holy Spirit; he demonstrates that evangelical soteriology reveals Trinitarian truth.

Timothy C. Tennent. *Invitation to World Missions: A Trinitarian Missiology for the Twenty-first Century* (Grand Rapids: Kregel, 2010).

Tennent, longtime missiologist, Chair of the Lausanne Theology Working Group, and current president of Asbury Seminary, masterfully unfolds a Trinitarian framework for missions. God the Father is the providential source, the Son the redemptive embodiment, and the Spirit the empowering presence of the *Missio Dei*. Serving as an introductory textbook, this resets the approach to global missions from a biblical Trinitarian perspective, in a way which is sensitive to cultural differentiations of Christian expression.

Leonardo Boff. *A Trindade, a sociedade e a libertação*. 3ª ed (Petrópolis RJ: Vozes, 1987).

Leonardo Boff. *Trinity and Society*, trans. Paul Burns (Tunbridge Wells, Kent, UK: Burns & Oates; and Maryknoll, New York: Orbis, 1988).

Boff, a liberation theologian, builds on the thinking of Jürgen Moltmann to elaborate a social Trinitarianism applied to societal and ecclesial relations; from Trinity he argues for a democratic and egalitarian society—this within Brazilian and Roman Catholic contexts. While the book creatively explores theological horizons, Boff intimates that the Spirit hypostatically incarnated in Mary, and he echoes Pierre Teilhard de Chardin's eschaton in which God inhabits the world as his own body, a hypostatic union with creation (or 'Christian pantheism'). Translated into several languages.

Athanasius. *On the Incarnation: The Treatise De Incarnatione Verbi Dei,* translated and edited by a Religious of C. S. M. V. Intro. C. S. Lewis. Revised edition (Crestwood NY: St. Vladimir's Seminary Press, 1998).

No work is more powerful in the articulation of early Trinitarianism than Athanasius' *On the Incarnation: The Treatise De Incarnatione Verbi Dei.* The writing itself stands as a positive, simply-worded, deeply profound statement of Trinitarian faith, 'a masterpiece' (C. S. Lewis), especially Chapters 3–5 (¶ 11–32; pp. 37–64). From this seminal piece (c. AD 318) flow themes elaborated far more thoroughly in the ecumenical councils that follow.
Available at http://www.worldinvisible.com/library/athanasius/incarnation/incarnation.c.htm

John Owen. *Of Communion with God the Father, Son, and Holy Ghost* (1657).

John Owen's (1616–1683) *Of Communion with God the Father, Son, and Holy Ghost* (1657), long a classic of puritan Trinitarian devotion, defends the truth that believers may properly worship and have fellowship with each Person of the Godhead. Such 'distinct communion' with a Person of the Trinity is never exclusive to that Person, but is to be enjoyed within the framework of how the Triune God has been revealed in Scripture. Owen's original work was strongly contested by some in his day, but has attracted fresh interest within the renaissance of Trinitarian studies. The full edition is available free as a pdf from the Christian Classics Ethereal Library. A similar edition is Kelly M. Kapic and Justin Taylor (eds), *John Owen, Communion with the Triune God* (Wheaton Illinois: Crossway, 2007).
Available at http://www.ccel.org/o/owen/communion

Jason S. Sexton. 'The State of the Evangelical Trinitarian Resurgence,' *Journal of the Evangelical Theological Society* 54, No. 4 (Dec 2011): 787–807.

Sexton provides a current panorama of evangelical North Atlantic Trinitarian thought and exploration over the last 25 years. He approaches the discussion through eight categories: 1) renewed patristic scholarship; 2) social Trinitarianism; 3) moratorium on subordinationism; 4) interdisciplinary philosophical concerns; 5) Trinitarian biblical theology; 6) Trinitarian theological interpretation of Scripture; 7) Trinitarian ecclesiology (worship, pastoral theology, mission); and 8) Christ-centeredness. The author suggests that evangelicals are moving ahead of non-evangelical counterparts in Trinitarian scholarship with (i) renewed research in biblical exegesis, (ii) early church tradition, and (iii) careful ethical and global applications.

Scott J. Horrell. 'In the Name of the Father, Son, and Holy Spirit: Toward a Trinitarian Worldview.' *Bibliotheca Sacra* 166 (April-June 2009) pp. 131-46.

The article outlines how Trinitarian confession shapes a Christian worldview amidst atheism, pantheism, and mono-personal theism. Designed for trans-cultural dialogue, the article begins by conceiving of God before creation. It then discusses how God as Trinity informs understanding of the *Imago Dei* in us as individual persons and in community. Issues of divine justice, forgiveness, and God as related to time and space are briefly addressed. Horrell gives us a panorama of Trinitarian applications, with the Nicene Creed perceived as the central unifying doctrine of Christian faith.

http://www.desiringgod.org/resource-library/articles/what-is-the-doctrine-of-the-trinity
http://bible.org/article/trinity-trinity-god
http://en.wikipedia.org/wiki/Trinity

John Piper's website Desiring God offers related articles and sermons. Matt Perman's 'What is the Trinity?' (2006) provides a succinct statement of the biblical, classical doctrine of the Trinity in four pages. The text carefully divides true from false concepts of the one God in three Persons, in a non-pejorative manner.

Likewise, Bible.org provides a sizeable archive of articles on the Godhead (about 550 in several languages), all from an evangelical perspective. 'The Trinity (Triunity) of God' (1997) (Spanish 'La Trinidad') by J. Hampton Keathley, III, is a 17-page biblical overview addressing problems raised by non-Trinitarians. For graduate students unversed in biblical Trinitarian arguments, these articles help establish a basic framework, especially where contentions of Jehovah's Witnesses and other sects arise.

The Wikipedia 'Trinity' (2012) English-language article addresses the biblical foundations and the historical development of Christian Trinitarianism. Entries in other languages may be less reliable. The 'Trinity' article is relatively balanced and ecumenical in addressing classical Christian faith as well as non-Trinitarian arguments. Using the ESV Bible (with links) the article is roughly 37 pages in length with Trinitarian art, 149 endnotes from an eclectic variety of sources, and multiple external links, many to evangelical sites. Some inaccuracies exist, not all the content is clear or current, and considerable attention is given to non-Trinitarian arguments (including Islam). Cautious use is encouraged.

THE CAPE TOWN CONFESSION OF FAITH

UNIT 5

PART I • SECTION 6
Our Love for the Word

Derek Thomas. '12 Keys to Spiritual Maturity, #6: In Love with Scripture.' A sermon on 2 Timothy 3:10-17, preached at the First Presbyterian Church, Jackson, Mississippi, USA, on July 15, 2001. Available online at: http://www.fpcjackson.org/resources/sermons/Derek%27s_SERMONS/12%20Keys/key6.htm

There is nothing like a sermon to exhort Christians to love God's Word, and this Lord's Day message by Dr. Derek Thomas gives its listeners just that. The message progresses through an exposition of the key text of 2 Timothy 3:10-17, pointing out that the Bible is the Word, the Word reveals who Jesus is, and the Word equips and sustains God's people.

Charles H. Spurgeon. 'Psalm 119: Exposition,' in Spurgeon's *Treasury of David*. Available online starting at: http://www.ewordtoday.com/comments/spurgeon/psalm119exposition1.htm

Psalm 119 is the most substantial portion of Scripture given to lauding the unsurpassed value of God's Word in governing the lives of God's people. Charles Spurgeon's verse-by-verse expositions drive readers to be filled with awe, passion, and love for the Word spoken of throughout the psalm with a wealth of images, metaphors, warnings, and exhortations.

Kwame Bediako. *Jesus in African Culture: A Ghanaian Perspective* (Accra, Ghana: Asempa Publishers, 1990). Also available in Kwame Bediako, *Jesus in African Culture: The Christian Gospel in African History and Experience*. Theological Reflections from the South Series (Yaoundé, Cameroun: Éditions Clé and Akropong-Akuepem, Ghana: Regnum Africa, 2000),
pp. 20-33. Note especially the final section, 'Reading and hearing the Word of God in our own language,' pp. 43-46 (pp. 32-33 in 2000 edition).

Kwame Bediako's brief but profound piece points to the central importance of hearing, loving, and working through the implications of God's Word in one's own mother tongue. We as God's people love God and his Word most deeply when God speaks to the depths of our inner being, as well as to the true character of our socio-religious setting, in our indigenous, vernacular languages.

Reginald T. Brooks. 'Thanks to God Whose Word Was Spoken,' 1954.

Brooks wrote this hymn for the 150th anniversary of the British and Foreign Bible Society. The hymn thanks God for how the Word has come to us through creation, Christ, the Bible (including as translated into our various languages), and the Holy Spirit. Available online at
http://www.hymnary.org/text/thanks_to_god_whose_word_was_spoken

PART I • SECTION 7
Our Love for the World

Catherine de Padilla. 'Love,' in John Corrie (ed) *Dictionary of Mission Theology: Evangelical Foundations* (Downers Grove, Illinois: IVP, 2007), pp. 212-214.

This warmly-written entry progresses through 'The first and great commandment', 'Love is the outworking of the relationship of the believer with the Triune God,' and 'The great commandment and the great commission.' Padilla cites Matthew 28:18-20, Luke 10:25-37, Micah 6:8, and 2 Corinthians 5:14. The summation of the article is that 'Love, then, becomes the *motivation*, the *model* and the *method* of the holistic, integral mission of the church.'

C. B. Hogue. *Love Leaves No Choice: Life-style Evangelism* (Waco, Texas: Word Books, 1976).

Toyohiko Kagawa. *Love the Law of Life.* Trans. by J. Fullerton Gressitt (Philadelphia, *Pennsylvania*: The John G. Winston Company, 1929).

These books take two different approaches to the theme of Christian love, but both exhort Christians to have love as their basic motivation for life and service. Hogue points Jesus' followers to the compulsion love gives to share the gospel of Jesus Christ. Kagawa points to the all-encompassing nature of love as the way of relating to God and to others.

David J. Bosch. *Transforming Mission: Paradigm Shifts in Theology of Mission.* American Society of Missiology Series, No. 16, Series Ed Comm. Chair, James Scherer (Maryknoll, New York: Orbis Books, 1991), pp. 286-288 (292-295 in Twentieth Anniversary Edition, 2011).

David Bosch, the eminent South African missiologist, in his monumental *Transforming Mission*, includes a section entitled 'Missionary Motifs in the Enlightenment: Constrained by Jesus' Love?' Bosch describes how love gradually became a dominant motif in the motivation for modern missions. John Wesley, Count Zinzendorf and the Moravians, and others are cited for their sacrificial love for Christ and for people throughout the world.

THE CAPE TOWN CONFESSION OF FAITH

UNIT 6

Part I • Section 8
The Gospel

Darrell L. Bock. *Recovering the Real Lost Gospel: Reclaiming the Gospel as Good News* (Nashville: Broadman and Holman, 2010).

This work is a biblical theological study of the concept of the gospel. It roots the gospel in the covenant promises of God to redeem the world. It shows how the gift of life in the indwelling Spirit, coming from the Messiah, is the core of the gospel message, running from John the Baptist, to Jesus, to Peter, to Paul, to John. It contends that the cross and Jesus' death for sin is the hub for the gospel, making possible the life that comes through the gift of the Spirit. It argues that Baptism and the Lord's Supper show key elements of the gospel, included in the idea of the Kingdom Jesus preached. It discusses how faith, repentance and turning are images to describe a proper response to the gospel. The gospel has individual, corporate and cosmic dimensions. The gospel is not about therapy, not about merely dodging a horrible fate of judgment, nor just a transaction; it is entry into a journey with God as by his grace we are reconnected to live life as God designed his creatures to live it.

Gerhard Friedrich. *'Euangélion'* in *Theological Dictionary of the New Testament*. Gerhard Kittel and Gerhard Friedrich (eds). 1 vol. (Grand Rapids, Michigan: Eerdmans, 1985), pp. 269-73.

This short article discusses the lexical usage of the term both in Scripture and the larger culture. It notes usage as general good news in the OT, and as news for victory or in the imperial cult, in general Greek language. The NT use is dominated by Jesus in the gospels, and by Paul elsewhere. Paul ties it mostly to a specific message about Jesus as the Promised One; his death for our sins as an eschatological event; and as the means of revealing God's justifying righteousness, combining judgment and grace. Christ is present in it. Faith arises through it, and is directed to it.

Greg Gilbert. *What is the Gospel?* (Wheaton: Crossway, 2010).

This work is a presentation of the gospel focused on the work of the cross. Working initially from Romans, Gilbert shows how the gospel deals with our rebellion against God, and with the problem of sin, and how it calls for the need for faith. He argues three other gospel messages are not the whole gospel: Jesus is Lord; Creation-Fall-Redemption-consummation; and cultural transformation.

Scot McKnight. *The King Jesus Gospel: The Original Good News Revisited* (Grand Rapids: Zondervan, 2011).

This work argues that there are two gospels in our public square and most current preaching has strayed from the original gospel. It distinguishes between a 'salvation culture' where the key idea in the gospel is to get saved from sin (see Gilbert above), and a 'gospel culture,' where the gospel covers not just salvation but the rule of God in Christ, completing the story of Israel in Scripture and touching on the entirety of creation. The gospel is about more than 'my salvation and me'. It is tied to the message of Jesus and the kingdom. Jesus is Messiah of Israel, Lord over all, and Davidic Savior. The call of the gospel is to confess this figure, embrace him and his work by faith, and enter into his alternative empire/community.

Richard Stearns. *The Hole in Our Gospel* (Nashville: Thomas Nelson, 2009).

Stearns argues: 'being a Christian, or follower of Jesus, requires much more than just having a *personal* and transforming relationship with God. It entails a *public* and transforming relationship to the world.' The gospel calls us to compassion and justice. We are to proclaim the good news and *be* the good news; to love God, love our neighbor and make disciples who will do the same. The book discusses poverty, disease and other key humanitarian needs as matters the church should address alongside the message of salvation. There is a challenge to examine how churches use their resources, and where resources are directed.

John Webster. 'Gospel,' in *Dictionary for Theological Interpretation of the Bible*. Kevin J. Vanhoozer, Craig G. Bartholomew, Daniel J. Treier, N. T. Wright (eds). (Grand Rapids: Baker, 2005), 263-64.

This short article defines the gospel as tied to salvation and 'the comprehensive reordering of God's relation to humankind'. It notes the OT background to the concept as in the LXX version of Isaiah 40:9; 52:7 and Nahum 1:15 (= 2:1 LXX). It points to a new eschatological stage of creaturely time. It results in renewed fellowship with God with the human correlate being the presence of faith.

D. A. Carson and Timothy Keller (eds). *The Gospel As Center: Renewing Our Faith and Reforming Our Ministry Practices* (Wheaton: Crossway, 2012).

This collection of essays comes from members of the Gospel Coalition. It works through each of the following: gospel-centered ministry, truth, creation, sin and fall, the plan of God, the gospel, justification, the Holy Spirit, the kingdom of God, the church, baptism and the Lord's Supper, and the restoration of all things. It concludes with confessional statements of the Coalition. It presents a gospel centered on Jesus with a balance between proclamation and practice as the way the church witnesses to this message.

PART I • SECTION 9
Our Love for God's People

Dietrich Bonhoeffer. *Life Together: A Discussion of Christian Fellowship*, trans. John W. Doberstein (New York: Harper & Row, 1954).

Bonhoeffer's classic offers great insights on loving God's people, and on the privilege of living in fellowship with other Christians. It opens readers' eyes to the Christian community as a source of incomparable joy, blessing, and strength. It points out why many believers cannot appreciate God's intended fellowship, and provides practical ways they can enjoy Christian community. Readers will be inspired to love other believers and to see the Christian community in a new dimension.

Gerald L. Sittser. *Love One Another: Becoming the Church Jesus Longs For*, 2nd ed (Downers Grove, Illinois: IVP, 2008).

Wayne Jacobsen and Clay Jacobsen. *Authentic Relationships: Discovering the Lost Art of 'One Anothering'* (Grand Rapids, Michigan: Baker, 2003).

Both books offer biblically-grounded reasons to love one another. They expose the deepest treasures of what it means to be part of God's family and expound a New Testament theology of 'one anothering'. Sittser encourages Christians to love across our differences in the church. The many differences can make the command of loving one another seem almost impossible, but this book proves it is possible. The Jacobsens have a similar focus but also help to reflect on building and developing friendships with other believers beyond church. By putting discussion questions in each chapter, readers can reflect on what they have read. This book is also useful for small groups.

These resources can be used in a biblical theology class, or a practical theology class; they give practical examples of how to apply the principles of 'one anothering.'

Chuck Miller. *The Spiritual Formation of Leaders: Integrating Spirituality and Leadership Development* esp. Chapters 5; 9-14 (Maitland, Florida: Xulon Press, 2007).

Larry Kreider and Jimmy Seibert. *The 3 Loves: The Three Passions at the Heart of Christianity* esp. section on 'Loving His People' (Ventura, California: Regal, 2010).

Christians are called to love Jesus/God, God's people, and the broken world. Both titles equip believers to love fellow-Christians, as they love God and firmly abide in Christ. In addition, Miller explores the nature of God's people, the church, and engages the inevitable challenges of living in the Christian community. Kreider and Seibert explain how loving God's people is expressed through discipleship, especially through mentoring. Readers will appreciate the real-life illustrations.

PART I • SECTION 10
Global Mission

David Barrett, George Kurian, Todd Johnson (eds). *World Christian Encyclopaedia*, 2 vols. (Oxford University Press, 2001).

David Barrett, Todd Johnson (eds). *World Christian Trends*, AD30-2200 (William Carey Library, Pasadena, California, 2001).

Todd Johnson and Kenneth Ross (eds). *Atlas of Global Christianity*. (Edinburgh: Edinburgh University Press, 2009).

> The first volume of the *World Christian Encyclopaedia* looks at the world by countries and by continent; the second by religions, peoples, languages, cities and topics. The data in the first volume formed the initial figures for the *World Christian Database* [WCD], now housed (with the World Religion Database) at Gordon Conwell, at the Center for the Study of Global Christianity, under the Directorship of Dr Todd Johnson. The *World Christian Encyclopaedia* data covers the years 1900, 1970, 1990, 1995, 2000 and 2025, with 1970 and 1995 being the pivotal years. The WCD is updated every five years.

> The world database, begun by David Barrett in the 1960s, has been foundational for global data. It was an enormous achievement. His original denominational groupings have become outmoded because of the growth of Christianity especially in the Global South. His definition of 'evangelical' omits those whom others would include (such as many Pentecostal and charismatic Christians).

> The *Atlas of Global Christianity* builds on the *World Christian Database* to give data from 1910 to 2010 and to 2050. There are many maps and essays on key subjects. It breaks down all the data into the 21 UN regions, rather than the six continents, but keeps the same denominations as in the *World Christian Encyclopaedia* – Anglicans, Catholics, Independents, Protestants, Orthodox and Marginals (ie Non-Trinitarian churches like the Mormons). It also gives extensive data on the global reach of the other major Religions, of which Agnosticism is treated as one. It also uses city information from Volume 2 of the *World Christian Encyclopaedia*.

Jason Mandryk and Patrick Johnstone (eds). *Operation World*, initially ed Patrick Johnstone and published in 1974, then in 1978, 1980, 1986, 1993, 2001; the seventh edition published in 2010 under the editorship of Jason Mandryk (WEC International and Biblica).

Patrick Johnstone. *The Future of Global Christianity* (WEC and Authentic, 2011).

> These two books come from the same stable. While up to the mid-1990s the databases behind *Operation World* and the *World Christian Encyclopaedia* were virtually identical, they began to diverge in the 1990s, partly because *Operation World* took a more generous definition of the world 'evangelical'. In 2010, *World Christian Encyclopaedia* said there were 300 million evangelicals worldwide, whereas *Operation World* said there were 550 million, so understanding exactly how these numbers are constructed, and the definitions behind them, is crucial.

> *Operation World* arises from a concern for mission, rather than to serve an academic readership. It gives a country-by-country analysis with political, economic, social, religious and demographic information, to provide context and 'soft data' for people to pray. It is produced in an economic paperback format.

> *The Future of Global Christianity* uses the database of *Operation World* with more detailed analysis and numerous diagrams, based on a high level of research, with informed explanations and suggestions for the future of mission.

Peter Brierley (ed). *World Churches Handbook.* (Lausanne and Christian Research, London, 1997).

Peter Brierley. *Global Religious Trends 2010 to 2020:* (Discussion document, January 2010).

Ronald Boyd-MacMillan. *Megatrends and the Persecuted Church* (Open Doors, 2011).

Pew Forum on Religion and Public Life. *Global Restrictions on Religion* (2011).

Barna Updates, http://www.barna.org

Global Mapping International, http://www.gmi.org

>   The *World Churches Handbook*, based on Patrick Johnstone's database, looks country by country at denominations, membership, and number of churches. It breaks global data down into the 10 broad Christian groups used in much UK analysis – Anglican, Baptist, Catholic, Independent, Lutheran, Methodist, Orthodox, Pentecostal, Presbyterian, and Others. It also has an index not available elsewhere, listing which denominations operate in which countries.
>
>   *Global Religious Trends* cites over 120 references. There are numerous books looking at certain sectors, such as *Global Pentecostalism*, by D E Miller and Tetsunao Yamamori (University of California Press, 2007), and *The New Faces of Christianity*. We also commend *The Next Christendom* and other books, by Philip Jenkins (Oxford University Press, 2006).

THE CAPE TOWN CALL TO ACTION

UNIT 7

PART 2 • SECTION IIA-1
Truth and the Person of Christ

Douglas Groothuis. *Christian Apologetics: A Comprehensive Case for Biblical Faith* (Downers Grove, ill. IVP Academic, 2011).

David A. Horner. *Mind Your Faith: A Student's Guide to Thinking and Living Well* (Downers Grove, Illinois: IVP Academic, 2011).

Andreas Köstenberger (ed). *Whatever Happened to Truth?* (Wheaton, Illinois: Crossway Books, 2005).

These books provide general introductions on understanding the gospel (and the Christian worldview) as truth which is objective, universal, and cosmic, as well as deeply personal and transformational in application and effect.

Groothuis introduces the Christian worldview as a matter of truth and knowledge (Chapter 4), describes the nature of truth (Chapter 6), and defends truth as objective (Chapter 7).

Horner gives a biblical and philosophical introduction to truth as propositional and personal (Chapter 3), clarifies its relation to belief, knowledge, and faith (Chapters 4 and 8), and casts a vision for engaging with the truth of the gospel broadly. He treats separately the mind (part 1), faith (part 2), and character (part 3).

Groothuis and Horner are accessible to a broadly educated audience. Köstenberger's edited volume is a source of more specific and technical articles concerning related biblical, theological, and philosophical issues (individual articles cited below).

Garret J. DeWeese and J. P. Moreland. *Philosophy Made Slightly Less Difficult: A Beginner's Guide to Life's Big Questions* (Downers Grove, Illinois: IVP, 2005).

Douglas Groothuis. *Truth Decay: Defending Christianity against the Challenges of Postmodernism* (Downers Grove, Illinois: IVP, 2000).

J. P. Moreland and William Lane Craig. *Philosophical Foundations for a Christian Worldview* (Downers Grove, Illinois: IVP Academic, 2003).

The above focus on the nature of truth at different levels of difficulty.

Horner (cited above) gives an accessible introduction as both propositional and personal, with an emphasis on truth as ultimately grounded and discovered in the Person of Jesus.

Groothuis provides an extensive account of biblical terms for truth (Chapter 3) and a defense of biblical truth as propositional (Chapter 4).

DeWeese and Moreland address philosophical issues surrounding truth in Chapter 3, as do Moreland and Craig at a more advanced level (Chapter 6). Also reflecting a more advanced discussion are several articles in the Köstenberger volume (cited above): J. P. Moreland defends truth as objective against postmodern objections ('Truth, Contemporary Philosophy, and the Postmodern Turn,' pp. 75-92), Kevin Vanhoozer explores the theological implications of truth as propositional and personal ('Lost in Interpretation? Truth, Scripture, and Hermeneutics,' pp. 93-129), and Andreas Köstenberger gives a biblical account of the Christological nature of truth ('What is Truth?' Pilate's Question in its Johannine and Larger Biblical Context,' pp. 19-51).

Michael Horton. 'The Good God Who Came Down.' *Christianity Today*, December 2011, pp. 24-29. Available online at http://www.christianitytoday.com/ct/2011/december/why-we-need-jesus.html

Timothy Keller. Free audio messages available at http://sermons2.redeemer.com/

Duane A. Litfin. *Conceiving the Christian College* (Grand Rapids, Michigan: Eerdmans, 2004).

Jonathan Lunde. *Following Jesus, the Servant King: A Biblical Theology of Covenantal Discipleship* (Grand Rapids, Michigan: Zondervan, 2010).

Litfin's book explores the integration of all knowledge within a Christian worldview. His approach, applied to Christian higher education, is helpful for the more general goal of exploring the Christocentric nature of truth and its cosmic implications. In Chapter 3, Litfin unpacks the biblical teaching (Colossians 1:15-17) that Jesus is Lord of all of life and thought. In Chapters 5 and 6, Litfin traces the implications of this cosmic vision for understanding and engaging truth. The writing, though scholarly, is accessible.

Lunde focuses more directly on the gospel task, applying the vision of Jesus Christ as Lord of all things to a biblical theology of the call to follow Jesus. Writing for a general church audience, Lunde casts a vision for understanding evangelism and discipleship within the twin biblical themes of Christ as reigning King and as representative, redeeming, and restoring Servant.

On a more popular level, Horton's article, the first in *Christianity Today*'s Global Gospel Project series, articulates the essential nature of the gospel in contrast to common religious and cultural substitutes. He stresses its universal scope and application as grounded in its historical particularity. Also at a popular level, Timothy Keller models (and teaches) gospel proclamation that reflects a richly biblical, corporate, and cosmic awareness.

Part 2 • Section IIA-2
Truth and the Challenge of Pluralism

James V. Brownson. *Speaking the Truth in Love: New Testament Resource for a Missional Hermeneutic* (Harrisburg, Pennsylvania: Trinity Press International, 1998).

Paul G. Heibert. *Missiological Implications of Epistemological Shifts: Affirming Truth in a Modern/Postmodern World* (Harrisburg, Pennsylvania: Trinity Press International, 1999).

Lesslie Newbigin. *Truth and Authority in Modernity* (Harrisburg, Pennsylvania: Trinity Press International, 1996).

Charles C. West. *Power, Truth, and Community in Modern Culture* (Harrisburg, Pennsylvania: Trinity Press International, 1999).

These four works are part of the series 'Christian Mission and Modern Culture' and engage their topics from the standpoint of the missional call.

Brownson explores how the Christian faith can be translated into new language and new cultural forms. He does so with an eye on the New Testament writers and how they attempted to interpret the gospel as it crossed cultural boundaries. Christians and Roman rule provide a case study and he concludes with a brief chapter on contemporary use of a missional hermeneutic.

Hiebert also looks at the problem of how Christian teaching is to be translated and communicated inter-culturally. In so doing he seeks to answer the question of how mission is to be done in an anti-colonial, postmodern era characterized by religious relativism and accusation of Christian imperialism. He embraces critical realism and restores emotions and moral judgments as essential parts of knowing.

Newbigin recognized how the Christian faith has become complicit in its relationship to secular western culture. His many books are intended to help release the faith from this Babylonian captivity. Speaking the gospel into contemporary society requires the Bible, tradition, reason and experience. In this book he speaks of how these resources are to be used and how they relate to one another.

West in three substantial chapters: The Gospel as Truth; The Gospel as Community; and The Gospel, the Power of God and Human Power, sets out a foundation for bearing witness to the economy of God amid the nations, rulers and powers in our culture.

Lesslie Newbigin. *The Gospel in a Pluralistic Society.* (Grand Rapids, Michigan: Eerdmans, 1989).

This important book brings together an academic perceptiveness with a wealth of mission experience. It serves to open up key issues around faithfulness to the gospel in a pluralistic setting. Whether one agrees or not, one is enriched by reading this work.

Douglas Groothuis. *Christian Apologetics: A Comprehensive Case for Biblical Truth*, especially Chapters 6 & 7 (Downers Grove: IVP, 2011).

Groothuis provides a sound biblical answer to the question, 'What is truth?' (Chapter 6). He then evaluates the most common tests for truth, paying careful attention to postmodern challenges. He ultimately defends a correspondence theory for truth, demonstrating its biblical validity while undercutting postmodern and pluralistic challenges. He moves on (Chapter 7) to biblical apologetic strategies, bolstered by cultural exegesis, for interacting with postmoderns. See also Chapter 23, which introduces the concepts of religious pluralism and a theology of religions.

Kevin J. Vanhoozer. *Is There a Meaning in This Text? The Bible, The Reader, and the Morality of Literary Knowledge* (Grand Rapids: Zondervan, 1998).

What happens when readers attempt to interpret texts for meaning without that believing truth can be communicated by authors in any authoritative sense? Vanhoozer examines, in detail, the current philosophical challenges to hermeneutics, including deconstruction and reader response strategies. He argues for the existence of authors as the controllers of meaning, that proper interpretation is not the creation of meaning, but the discovery of meaning intended by the author, and that readers have a moral obligation to read texts charitably and humbly, submitting to the meaning-controlling authority of that text's author. This is a critical book.

John M. Frame. *The Doctrine of the Knowledge of God* (Phillipsburg, New Jersey: P&R Publishing, 1987).

This excellent volume evaluates the many ways people attempt to justify truth claims. Frame's primary thesis is because God is the creator of mankind and the creator of the world, he has also created mankind to know something of the world. This can only be done coherently if we submit our thinking to the Lord Jesus Christ. The problem with many secular approaches to knowledge and the justification of truth claims is not that people are looking for truth in the wrong places, but that they are looking in those places faithlessly. See also John M. Frame, *The Doctrine of the Word of God* (Phillipsburg, New Jersey: P&R Publishing, 2010).

D. A. Carson. *The Gagging of God: Christianity Confronts Pluralism* (Grand Rapids: Zondervan, 1996; Leicester, UK: IVP, 1996).

Carson's *The Gagging of God* explores the philosophical and religious foundations of pluralism and alerts the church to the crisis of truth that such thinking creates. His solution is a robust dependence upon the Word of God, paying close attention to its biblical-theological storyline. Throughout, Carson maintains that Jesus Christ alone, among all other religious challengers, is truth. One must believe the gospel in order to be saved. Carson also offers insightful cultural exegesis and provides some explanation of and responses to religious pluralism, universalism, and inclusivism.

T. L. Miles. *A God of Many Understandings? The Gospel and a Theology of Religions* (Nashville, Tennessee: Broadman & Holman, 2010).

This evangelical theology of religions argues for the need for conscious faith in Christ in order to be saved. The question 'What about those who have never heard?' is answered with the biblical injunction, 'Go tell them!' Miles defines a Christian theology of religions, and develops a biblical theology of religions which demonstrates that both the Old and New Testaments were written in the context of religious pluralism. Miles evaluates and argues against pluralism (many paths lead to God), universalism (all will be saved), and inclusivism (one can be saved by the work of Christ without hearing and believing the gospel). The last chapter asks and answers questions regarding salvation and truth in other religions, interfaith dialogue, and interfaith cooperation in social justice causes.

David F. Wells. *Above All Earthly Powers: Christ in a Postmodern World* (Grand Rapids, Michigan: Eerdmans, 2005).

Wells exegetes the postmodern culture, and evaluates the Church's commitment to and presentation of the doctrine of Christ in that cultural milieu. Wells calls the church to hold courageously, wisely, and faithfully to the historic doctrine of Christ, even when the very concept of truth is disputed, let alone its particulars, and when the prevailing cultural ethos celebrates diversity for its own sake. A Christian must hold to Christ in contexts where religious pluralism is elevated as the way things ought to be. See also David F. Wells, *No Place for Truth: Or Whatever Happened to Evangelical Theology* (Grand Rapids, Michigan: Eerdmans, 1993).

Harold Netland. *Dissonant Voices: Religious Pluralism and the Question of Truth* (Grand Rapids, Michigan: Eerdmans, 1991).

Harold Netland. *Encountering Religious Pluralism: The Challenge to Christian Faith & Mission* (Downers Grove: IVP, 2001).

Netland is a theologically- and philosophically-astute missiologist. These two volumes cover the nature of truth claims by religious others, and normative Christian truth claims in a pluralistic context. Netland also treats apologetic and evangelistic strategies for encountering religious others. Netland, himself an evangelical, studied under the pluralist John Hick, so is well-acquainted with the arguments and the ethos of religious and philosophical pluralism. Netland traces the development of pluralism particularly responding to Hick, claiming him to be the most influential apologist for religious pluralism. Netland provides us with insights for developing a comprehensive evangelical theology of religions.

Ken Gnanakan. *Kingdom Concerns* (Bangalore: Theological Book Trust / Leicester: IVP 1990).

An introduction to God's mission alongside the concept of the Kingdom of God from an author in the Majority World, written from a majority world perspective. The study covers historical, biblical and theological insights that enable the reader to grasp the whole mission of God.

Lesslie Newbigin. *The Gospel in a Pluralist Society* (Grand Rapids, Michigan: Eerdmans, 1989).

Lesslie Newbigin, a highly-respected missionary to India and an influential ecumenical figure, provides a colorful analysis of contemporary culture and shows how Christians must more confidently affirm their faith in this context. Newbigin addresses pertinent questions recalling some vivid illustrations from his experience as a missionary.

John Hick and Paul Knitter (eds). *The Myth of Christian Uniqueness: Toward a Pluralistic Theology of Religions* (London: SCM Press, and Maryknoll, New York: Orbis Books, 1988/1989).

Twelve theologians, who shared in a conference in California, among them some well-known liberals, seek Christian perceptions of other faiths beyond exclusivism and inclusivism. The book makes a case for a pluralistic response. They propose a Copernican revolution – Christianity and God are no longer the center but a universal human search for and experience of salvation.

Gavin D'Costa. *Christian Uniqueness Reconsidered: The Myth of a Pluralistic Theology of Religions* (Maryknoll, New York: Orbis Books, 1990).

Gavin D'Costa brings together the contributions of fourteen outstanding scholars who address the argument that all religious traditions are 'equal'. This book is a response to Hick and Knitter. Some approaches do not totally negate other religious traditions.

Ken Gnanakan. *Proclaiming Christ in a Pluralistic Context* (Theological Book Trust, Bangalore, India, 2000).

Ken Gnanakan, writing from the context of India, where pluralism abounds in its Hindu culture, provides a response to such questions as: Is Christianity the only way? What about sincere followers of other religious faiths? How can we continue to proclaim Christ today? Gnanakan provides principles to guide in our theology of religions from a creation perspective.

John G. Stackhouse (ed). *No Other Gods Before Me? Evangelicals and the Challenge of World Religions* (Grand Rapids: Baker Academic, 2001).

Stackhouse brings together leading theologians from a variety of evangelical backgrounds to discuss Christian encounters with world religions. Questions addressed are - What are religions? Are non-Christian faiths legitimate means of accessing the divine? Is there divine revelation in non-Christian religions? Is the 'Jesus Story' found in other faith traditions? Contributors provide a careful theological, sociological, historical, and anthropological treatment of Christian interaction with people of other faiths.

Part 2 • Section IIA-3
The Workplace

R. Paul Stevens. *The Other Six Days: Vocation, Work and Ministry in Biblical Perspective* (Grand Rapids, Michigan: Eerdmans, 2000).

The author is professor emeritus of marketplace theology and leadership at Regent College, Vancouver, British Columbia, and adjunct professor at Bakke Graduate University, Seattle, Washington, and at Biblical Graduate School of Theology in Singapore. He is a key thinker and contributor to the theology of workplace ministry.

Stevens presents a strong argument that the clergy-laity division has no biblical basis. He encourages lay Christians to live out their faith in every sphere of life: home, work or society. He argues against the view that the clergy is called out for ministry while the rest are spectators. The role of the church is to equip people to do ministry in the workplace and at home. There are thought-provoking case studies and questions at the end of each chapter. The core idea is that every day of the week, and not just Sunday, is filled with spiritual meaning and significance to every follower of Christ, if we embrace our calling to serve him and his creation through all the gifts and skills at our disposal.

Gene Edward Veith Jr. *God at Work: Your Christian Vocation in All of Life* (Wheaton, Illinois: Crossway Books, 2002).

A key concept coming out of the Protestant Reformation was the priesthood of all believers. Veith writes, 'Every kind of work [including fathering and mothering] ... is an occasion for priesthood, for exercising a holy service to God and to one's neighbor.' Therefore, our vocations are meant to honor and enjoy God. Veith writes that God didn't establish secular work apart from the sacred. He designed everything as sacred.

Ed Silvoso. *Anointed for Business: How Christians Can Use Their Influence in the Marketplace to Change the World* (Ventura, California: Regal, 2002).

Ed Silvoso explains that every business is God's business. Through a study of the lives of the disciples and apostles of the New Testament, Silvoso shows how Jesus chose lay people to lead the early church while many continued to engage in jobs and businesses. For example Matthew is a tax collector, Luke a medical doctor, Dorcas a clothing designer, Peter a fisherman, Paul a tentmaker: the founders of the church were people whom we would encounter in the marketplace today. Silvoso calls upon the clergy and laity to break down the wall between commercial pursuit and service to God for revival in every sphere of society. He is especially interested in seeing a revival in the cities and believes the heart of the city is the marketplace. Our starting point for ministry should be the marketplace, and those best placed for the work are those already engaged in it.

Os Hillman. *The 9 to 5 Window: How Faith Can Transform the Workplace* (Ventura, California: Regal, 2005).

Os Hillman is a leading authority on marketplace ministry. This is a window into the move of God in the workplace, showing how God's people integrate their faith with their work life. Topics include facts on the current faith at work movement, how to bring the presence of God into the workplace, developing an intercessory prayer team at work, transforming the workplace, city, and nation for Christ. There is a Bible study guide at the end for small group study.

Patrick Lai. *Tentmaking: The Life and Work of Business as Missions* (Colorado Springs, Colorado: Authentic, 2005).

Patrick Lai draws from his own experience and from extensive research among 450 tentmakers laboring in the 10/40 window. Chapters deal with such issues as tentmaking vs. 'traditional' missions, types of tentmaking, preparing to be a tentmaker, evangelism and church planting, the tentmaker's personal life, women and tentmaking, the tentmaker and his children, the tentmaker and his home base, tentmaking tensions and conflicts. Appendices provide checklists, team guidelines, questions for short-term workers, church planting phases, and reflections on joining a missions agency team. Highly commended for those who want to learn about tentmaking in the 10/40 window.

Mark L Russell (ed). *Our Souls at Work: How Great Leaders Live Their Faith in the Marketplace* (Boise, Idaho: Russell Media, 2010).

Our Souls at Work is a compilation of insights and personal stories shared by 37 Christian leaders from corporate America. It is built around twelve themes: calling, leadership, character, success, money, stewardship, balance, disciplines, relationships, pluralism, ethics and giving. The book is organized by key topics. The contributors share their views on a given topic so that the reader gets the benefit of multiple viewpoints.

Mats Tunehag, Wayne McGee, and Josie Plummer (eds). *Business as Mission*.

Lausanne Occasional Paper #59. Lausanne BAM Paper 2004 (Produced by the first global think tank on BAM, and including the *Business as Mission Manifesto*. See also *Lausanne BAM Paper Discussion Guide*.

The Lausanne 2004 Forum Business as Mission (BAM) Issue Group worked for a year, addressing issues relating to God's purposes for work and business, the role of business people in church and missions, the needs of the world and the potential response of business. The group consisted of more than 70 people from all continents. Most came from a business background but there were also church and mission leaders, educators, theologians, lawyers and researchers.

For news and resources from the Second Global Think Tank, in partnership with Lausanne (2012–2013), see http://www.bamthinktank.org

(Also see below: BAM articles and papers in languages other than English.)

Bridget Adams and Manoj Raithatha. Building the Kingdom Through Business: A Mission Strategy for the 21st Century World. Available at http://www.instantapostle.com

This is a BAM book. If business shapes the world, how can we use it for good and for God? Against the background of international debate on business ethics and just societies, this looks at godly business in biblical, historic and practical ways. It includes advice on starting a business, and case studies of businesses making a difference.

For a BAM bibliography, go to http://www.businessasmission.com/books.html

A few samples:

C. Neal Johnson. *Business as Mission: A Comprehensive Guide to Theory and Practice* (Downers Grove: IVP, 2010).

Christian-led companies and business leaders do not automatically accomplish missional purposes in business strategy. BAM requires mastery of both the world of business and the world of missions, merging and contextualizing both into something significantly different than either alone. C. Neal Johnson offers the first comprehensive guide to business as mission for practitioners. He provides conceptual foundations for understanding BAM's unique place in global mission and prerequisites for engaging in it. Then he offers practical resources for how to do BAM, including strategic planning and step-by-step operational implementation. Drawing on a wide variety of BAM models, Johnson works through details of both mission and business realities, with an eye to such issues as management, sustainability and accountability.

Wayne Grudem. *Business for the Glory of God: The Bible's Teaching on the Moral Goodness of Business* (Wheaton: Crossway, 2003).

Can business activity be morally good and pleasing to God? Wayne Grudem introduces a novel concept: business itself glorifies God when it is conducted in a way that imitates God's character and creation. He shows that all aspects of business, including ownership, profit, money, competition, and borrowing and lending, glorify God because they are reflective of God's nature. See how your business, and your life in business, can be dedicated to God's glory.

Michael R. Baer. *Business as Mission: The Power of Business in the Kingdom of God* (Seattle: YWAM Publishing, 2006).

Christian business leaders have the chance to play a pivotal role in transforming society and spreading the gospel. Baer guides business leaders in developing the vital characteristics of a kingdom business - the kind of business that will free them to live fully integrated lives and lead organizations that significantly impact the world.

Steve Rundle and Tom Steffen. *Great Commission Companies: The Emerging Role of Business in Mission* (Downers Grove: IVP, 2011).

In this landmark book, economist Steve Rundle and missiologist Tom Steffen offer their paradigm for the convergence of business and missions - the Great Commission Company. It opens up new possibilities for missions-minded entrepreneurs and business people want to bring change, and do business to the glory of God. This revised and expanded edition provides new and updated case studies set in diverse contexts.

Doug Seebeck and Timothy Stoner. *My Business, My Mission: Fighting Poverty Through Partnerships* (Grand Rapids: CRC Publications, 2009).

My Business, My Mission tells the story of a movement that is changing the lives of tens of thousands of people in the most impoverished nations on earth. It is also transforming business people in the northern and southern hemispheres by exposing them to a revolutionary paradigm: the idea that God has called them into mission through business. Through the work of a remarkable organization called Partners Worldwide, North American business people and entrepreneurs in developing countries are joining together to fight poverty. Their mission is simple: to expand their businesses, create wealth, and provide jobs for the poor in Christ's name.

WEA-MC Journal Connections, BAM issue, fall 2009 contains articles on Business as Mission from thought leaders and practitioners from Asia, Africa, Latin America, Europe and North America.

http://www.weaconnections.com/Back-issues/Business-As-Mission.aspx

The articles include:

Case Study on BAM SME from Korea to Other Parts of Asia. *Joseph Lee*

Restoring People, Changing Businesses, Transforming Societies – A Case Study from Indonesia. *Julian Foe*

The Challenges and Opportunities For Business As Mission: A Perspective From Africa. *Dennis Tongoi*

Bossa Nova, the 'Beautiful Game' and Business as Mission (A Brazilian Perspective). *João Mordomo*

Larger-Sized Business as Mission (BAM) Companies. (Chinese Perspectives) *Dwight Nordstrom & Vince Liang*

Why Is Bangladesh Poor and Taiwan Rich? *Mats Tunehag & Peter Shaukat*

Business as Mission: Towards a Biblical and Practical Theology of Work and Business. *Bridget Adams*

Church, Missions and Business: Roles, Responsibilities, Tension and Synergies. *Peter Shaukat*

Human Trafficking: Business as Prevention and Restoration. *Jennifer Roemhildt Tunehag*

Ten Principles: BAM in areas of Prostitution and Trafficking. *Annie Dieselberg*

The Experiment in Integrated Mission – Business, Mission, and Social Transformation. *Trev Gregory*

The Mission of Business: CSR+. *Mats Tunehag*

Chickens, computers, and steel parts – Why business-based ministry is so effective. *Matt in Asia*

Video: *God is at work and He loves it!*

A 35-minute video looking at biblical models of the workplace. Stimulating as a discussion starter. Based on a sermon at Sarang Community Church, a Korean American mega church in Los Angeles.

Watch the video online at http://holywave.sarang.com/index.cfm?page=videos.cfm&catID=10&pg=1&vidCat=1

[BAM has articles and papers in the following languages: Arabic, Bahasa, Chinese, Farsi, Finnish, French, German, Korean, Portuguese, Russian, Spanish, Swedish, Turkish, Vietnamese: http://www.matstunehag.com/further-reading]

For another treatment of the issue, see Pope John Paul II in Centesimus annus 1991 on profit and capitalism.

Catherwood, Sir Fred. *Light, Salt and the World of Business* (*Didasko Files* series. Peabody, Massachusetts: Lausanne Library / Hendrickson. Revised ed. 2012). 32pp with discussion questions. A short, and highly stimulating class reader on how Christians can change society through a committed stance against corruption. Foreword by Paul Batchelor of Transparency International.

Paul Batchelor and Steve Osei-Mensah. Salt and Light. *Christians' role in combating corruption.* Presentation to the Government, Business and Academia (GBA) Think Tank at The Third Lausanne Congress.

http://conversation.lausanne.org/en/home/home/943/featured

> This paper, now part of the Lausanne Global Conversation, is written by two senior businessmen, both with wide global experience. It addresses the realities of corruption in all societies, with a robust evangelical response, and poses stimulating questions.

PART 2 • SECTION IIA-4
The Media

Lars Dahle. (June, 2010). 'Media Messages Matter: Christ, Truth and the Media' *Cape Town 2010 Advance Paper on Media and Technology*. See also the author's regular blog Media Messages Matters, on media awareness, media critique and media ministries and Christian apologetics. The material on Acts 17:16-34 as an apologetic model is especially relevant to this section in *Bearing witness to the truth of Christ in a pluralized, globalized world*.

Media and Technology: The Rainbow, The Ark & The Cross. [Lausanne Occasional Paper #48, 2004]

These two resources offer brief, accessible and comprehensive overviews of Christian engagement with the world of the media. Both emphasize the urgent need for such engagement locally, regionally, and globally. The Cape Town Advance Paper on Media and Technology introduces the three key categories of media awareness, media presence and media critique. It also focuses on the need to acknowledge a rich biblical view of truth (propositional, relational and experiential). Furthermore, Acts 17:16-34 is explored as a significant and representative biblical model for cultural engagement. The Lausanne Occasional Paper on Media and Technology (2004) with its case study approach complements The Cape Town Paper (2010). This practical approach is grounded in insightful reflections on media-specific, mission-specific and model-specific concerns. Thus, the reader is introduced to the whole area of media ministries.

Paul Marshall, Lela Gilbert, Roberta Green-Ahmanson (eds). *Blind Spot: When Journalists Don't Get Religion* (Oxford / New York: Oxford University Press, 2009). These key concerns are regularly and professionally covered at The Media Project. Go to http://www.themediaproject.org

Tony Watkins. *Focus: The Art & Soul of Cinema* (Milton Keynes: Authentic Media, 2007). Also available as an ebook. The author is editor of the popular weekly Damaris resource CultureWatch which 'explores the message behind the media'.

EngagingMedia.info – a website set up by Lars Dahle and the Media & Technology Team in connection with The Cape Town Congress to help Christians develop practical media awareness skills in relation to media messages, with a specific emphasis on worldviews.

The Marshall and Watkins books are insightful contributions to a Christian perspective on media awareness and critique. This underemphasized area urgently needs to be addressed by theologians, pastors, youth workers, and other Christian educators. *Blind Spot* explores the news media world and its lack of understanding of religion in general and Christian faith especially. *Focus* breaks new ground in its emphasis on a worldview approach to the understanding and critique of fictional film and cinema. Watkins helps the reader to form critical reflections on truth, identity and meaning, within an understanding of the genres, motifs and themes of contemporary movies. *The Engaging Media website* applies the same worldview approach to a wide selection of media messages, including news, documentary, novels, music, and comics.

PART 2 • SECTION IIA-5
The Arts

Jeremy S. Begbie (ed). *Beholding the Glory: Incarnation through the Arts.* (Grand Rapids: Baker Book House, 2000).

Ned Bustard (ed). *It Was Good: Making Art to the Glory of God*, 2nd edition (Baltimore Maryland: Square Halo Books, 2006).

Begbie serves as an introductory reflection on literature, poetry, dance, icons, sculpture, and music—and a mid-level theological exploration into the relationship between these art forms and the theme of the incarnation. While often working in the area of the arts, Begbie is a theologian first.

It Was Good affirms creation and creativity. The authors explore the arts through such themes as beauty, presence, creativity, glory, mission, and truthfulness.

Hilary Brand and Adrienne Chaplin. *Art and Soul: Signposts for Christians in the Arts*, 2nd edition (Downers Grove, Illinois: IVP, 2001).

Steve Turner. *Imagine: A Vision for Christians in the Arts* (Downers Grove, Illinois.: IVP, 2001).

Calvin Seerveld. *Bearing Fresh Olive Leaves: Alternative Steps in Understanding Art* (Toronto: Tuppence Press, 2000).

Each addresses questions and themes related to the faith and the arts. Brand and Chaplin speak to how art fits within a Christian worldview drawing on the doctrines of creation, fall and redemption. They engage examples from both traditional and contemporary art while probing such issues as art and worship, the nature of art and the vocation of the artist.

Seerveld sees art as a sign of hope in a broken world and invites the faith community to attend to the arts and cultivate the aesthetic life as integral to our call to faithfulness. Steve Turner explores the dualism so often present in Christian understanding of the world and discerns how it impacts our reception of the arts. Keen insight and thoughtful commentary are found in all of these works.

All speak from a reformed perspective.

Hans Rookmaaker. *Art Needs no Justification* (Downers Grove, Illinois: IVP, 1978).

This brief work from the Dutch art historian provides a good foundation for thinking about how the arts fit within a Christian understanding of the world. As those who bear the image of God we are destined to exercise the creative gift, so there is no need to justify the calling to make art.

Andy Crouch. *Culture Making: Recovering our Creative Calling* (Downers Grove, Illinois: IVP, 2008).

This work does not focus on art, but clearly articulates a call to be 'culture makers', one expression of which is art. Crouch demonstrates that the call has strong support in scripture and requires intentional effort by all within the faith community – not least among those who do mission.

John W. De Gruchy. *Christianity, Art, and Transformation* (Cambridge: Cambridge University Press, 2001).

De Gruchy, rooted in his South African context, explores transformation of society through the powerful relationship of the arts and Christianity. Major themes include the power of images; aesthetics and ethics; the redemptive capacity of beauty; aesthetic existence and Christian discipleship; and the role of art in the public square and in the life of the church. Art can be a catalyst for cultural change. We sense the power of beauty and its capacity for bringing change, as its depiction of injustice and oppression leads to social upheaval. Here is art with a prophetic edge.

Makoto Fujimura. *Refractions: A Journey of Faith, Art, and Culture* (Colorado Springs, Colorado: NavPress, 2009).

Makoto Fujimura is a notable Japanese-American contemporary artist, and founder of the International Arts Movement. *A Journey of Faith, Art, and Culture* is a stirring reflection and meditation on his love of culture, his love of community and his love of God. Woven throughout are the themes of peace-making and community-building. The book itself is a notable piece of craftsmanship and art.

Journal IMAGE: Art, Faith, Mystery.

A fine literary journal situated within the gap of art and religion. Includes quality articles, stories, poems and reviews in the arts from a Christian perspective. http://www.imagejournal.org

W. David O. Taylor (ed). *For the Beauty of the Church: Casting a Vision for the Arts* (Grand Rapids: Baker Books, 2010).

A collection of essays by authors including Andy Couch, Eugene Peterson, David Taylor, Lauren Winner, and John Witvliet explore the mobilizing of artists for theological reflection, formation, and worship. John Witvliet asks how art can serve the corporate worship of the church. Eugene Peterson recounts his own experience of how artists shape pastoral identity. Taylor has an essay on the dangers of art-making in the church. This book will be helpful both for those initiating an arts presence in the church as well as those seasoned in their work with artists. These essays think through the benefits and risks of including arts within the fabric of the church and Christian ministry.

Catherine Kapikian. *Art in the Service of the Sacred* (Nashville: Abingdon Press, 2006).

Kapikian offers encouragement to take seriously the role of visual art in worship. The book serves as a timely reminder of the value of the aesthetic in the corporate life of the church, and particularly in our desire to encounter God.

Chaim Potok. *My Name is Asher Lev* (New York: Fawcett Columbine, 1972).

Dorothy L. Sayers. *The Mind of the Maker* (London: Religious Book Club, 1942).

Jewish author Chaim Potok tells the story of a devout young Jewish artist Asher Lev, driven by the need to paint and draw. Both the external pressure and the inner conflict he experiences between his faith and his art is a story familiar to many within the Christian community. His resolution may be instructive for those who experience this conflict.

Dorothy Sayers takes us on a journey of theological understanding by opening up the subject of divine creation and making links to the human capacity to create.

Jeremy S. Begbie. *Resounding Truth: Christian Wisdom in the World of Music* (Grand Rapids Michigan: Baker Academic 2007).

William Dyrness. *Visual Faith: Art, Theology, and Worship in Dialogue* (Grand Rapids Michigan: Baker Academic 2001).

Todd E. Johnson and Dale Savidge. *Performing the Sacred: Theology and Theatre in Dialogue* (Grand Rapids Michigan: Baker Academic, 2009).

Robert K. Johnston. *Reel Spirituality: Theology and Film in Dialogue* (Grand Rapids Michigan: Baker Academic, 2000).

These offer theologically-informed introductions to artistic genres. In addition to some history, they provide up-to-date illustrations of the art form, framing arguments with biblical support, and offering practical advice.

Gesa Elsbeth Thiessen (ed). *Theological Aesthetics: A Reader* (Grand Rapids: Eerdmans, 2004).

Excerpts from Augustine, Meister Eckhart, Luther, Calvin, Wesley, Kant, Kierkegaard, Tillich, Barth, von Balthasar, Begbie and others, on the relationship between theology, the church, and the arts. The writings, wide in scope, cover the intersection of religion and the arts, beauty and revelation, the vision of God, artistic and divine creation, meanings of signs and symbols, worship, liturgy, the relationship of words and images, and the role of icons. A valuable resource.

Nicholas Wolterstorff. *Art in Action: Toward a Christian Aesthetic* (Grand Rapids, Michigan: Eerdmans, 1980).

Wolterstorff, a respected Christian philosopher, writes in an approachable way, suggesting works of art are instruments and objects of action, linked to the fabric of human purpose. The arts have a variety of public roles, whence the place and presence of artists and their offerings in our Christian communities.

Lausanne Occasional Paper #46. *Redeeming the Arts,* http://www.lausanne.org

Connections September 2010, *Arts and Mission*, Magazine of the World Evangelical Alliance, Mission Commission http://www.weaconnections.com

> Both documents were shaped in the context of mission. LOP #46 is a sustained discussion of arts and theology, arts and discipleship in the church and arts and the transformation of culture. The *Connections* issue is a collection of articles that speaks to arts in the practice of mission with reflective pieces on the importance of engaging the arts as a resource for mission.

Several quality bibliographies have been created in the intersection of the Arts, Theology, and the Church. They can be found at:

> http://www.st-andrews.ac.uk/itia/reading/arts.html
>
> http://civa.org/resources/civa-recommends
>
> http://iws.edu/IWS/Pdfs/Bibliography.pdf
>
> http://ai.clm.org/bibliographies/fineartstheory.html

PART 2 • SECTION IIA-6
Science and Technology

John Dyer. *From the Garden to the City: The Redeeming and Corrupting Power of Technology* (Grand Rapids: Kregel, 2011).

A starter book tracing the use and significance of technology from biblical history through modern times, and showing how culture, faith, and technology interact. Dyer (a web developer with a seminary degree) highlights the redemptive importance of technology as well as the unintended problems it often brings.

Tim Challies. *The Next Story: Life and Faith after the Digital Explosion* (Grand Rapids: Zondervan, 2011).

Challies, a major blogger, sets up a basic framework for looking at technology then addresses several key areas like distraction, communication, identity, author, and privacy.

Heidi Campbell. *When Religion Meets New Media* (London: Routledge, 2010).

This book is more academic in its tone and language. Campbell researched how Christians, Jews, and Muslims approach technology for almost twenty years. Her case studies offer valuable insight that is more helpful than the anecdotes and opinions found in other books.

Eric Brende. *Better Off: Flipping the Switch on Technology* (New York: HarperCollins, 2004).

Brende spent 18 months living 'off the grid', as a pumpkin farmer with a Mennonite community. He is perhaps too negative in his views of technology, but the book provides good insight into the pace of our daily lives which surfaces through an extended narrative.

Nicolas Carr. *The Shallows: What the Internet Is Doing to Our Brains* (New York: W. W. Norton & Co., 2011).

The author of the oft-cited *Atlantic* article, 'Is Google Making Us Stupid?' looks at neurological research on how the brain is changing in response to internet usage and related technologies like text messages. He argues that it detracts from our ability to do 'deep reading'. This could have significant bearing on the next generation of Christian teachers.

T. David Gordon. *Why Johnny Can't Preach: The Media Have Shaped the Messengers* (Phillipsburg, New Jersey: P&R Publishing, 2009).

Gordon, a musician teaches Greek and studies media ecology. He applies media theory to the practice of preaching clearly, and argues that many of today's preachers have been so shaped by media, they often fail to communicate God's word faithfully.

Nigel Cameron. *Scoping the Future: Twitter, NASA, SXSW and other questions* (Kindle ebook, 2012).

Nigel Cameron and Charles Colson (eds). *Human Dignity in the Bio-tech Century: A Christian Vision for Public Policy*, 2004.

Nigel M. de S. Cameron and M. Ellen Mitchell (eds). *Nanoscale: Issues and Perspectives for the Nano Century* (Hoboken, New Jersey: John Wiley, 2007).

Nigel Cameron is recommended for students who want to extend their thinking into the critical areas of public policy. Cameron, an academic theologian, and founding president of the Biocentre (London) and the Center for Policy on Emerging Technologies (Washington, DC) engages issues of innovation and the human future with a robust intellect and an evangelical worldview.

Part 2 • Section IIA-7
Public Arenas

J. M. Kouzes and B.Z. Posner. *The Leadership Challenge* (San Francisco: Jossey Bass, 1990, Fourth edition, 2008).

J. M. Kouzes and B.Z. Posner. *Credibility: How Leaders Gain and Lose It, Why People Demand It* (San Francisco: Jossey Bass, 2003, Revised edition, 2011).

Truth and integrity are foundational for Christian witness. If you stand on truth and integrity, nothing else matters; if you don't have truth and integrity, nothing else matters. Kouzes and Posner's secular books on the challenge of leadership stress that without integrity and credibility leadership is not possible.

Henry Cloud. *Integrity: The Courage to Meet the Demands of Reality* (New York: HarperCollins, 2006).

Fred Catherwood. *Light, salt and the world of business: Good practice can change nations* (*Didasko Files* series. Peabody, Massachusetts: Lausanne Library / Hendrickson. Revised ed. 2012).

Sir Fred Catherwood, a senior figure in UK government and business, brings out clearly that honesty works, and prospers. This short text (32pp) shows the inter-relation of government, business and academia, and the centrality of the university in forming and informing a nation's leaders. Highly commended title in a distinctive series.

http://www.lausanne.org/docs/capetown2010/summaries/P218-Truth.pdf

Christian leaders are not exempt from dishonesty and corruption pervading all cultures. The presentation of Chris Wright on 'Calling the Church of Christ Back to Humility, Integrity and Simplicity' at the Cape Town Congress is an excellent summary of the problem and how it can be solved. Os Guinness also spoke on these issues in his presentation on 'Making the Case for the Truth of Christ in a Pluralistic, Globalized World.'

Lesslie Newbigin. *Foolishness to the Greeks: The Gospel and Western Culture* (Grand Rapids, Michigan: Eerdmans, 1986).

Lesslie Newbigin. *The Gospel in a Pluralist Society* (Grand Rapids, Michigan: Eerdmans, 1989).

Lesslie Newbigin, a renowned thinker, and missionary in South India for 40 years, looks at how biblical authority should influence and shape our entire existence, in both Western and non-Western cultures.

Harry Blamires. *The Christian Mind: How Should a Christian Think?* (Vancouver: Regent College, 2005).

Harry Blamires. *On Christian Truth* (Vancouver: Regent College, 2005).

Stanley Grenz. *A Primer on Postmodernism* (Grand Rapids, Michigan: Eerdmans, 1996).

'Just do it … don't bother about the consequences' is a direct outcome of postmodern thinking. Harry Blamires focuses on how a Christian should think differently, and what he should believe. Stanley Grenz focuses on how Christians should proclaim the truth and the gospel to a postmodern generation.

Nancy Pearcey. *Total Truth: Liberating Christianity from Its Cultural Captivity* (Wheaton, Illinois: Crossway, 2004).

Pearcey, much influenced by her teacher, Francis Schaeffer, at L'Abri, emphasizes the practicality of a coherent Christian worldview, and the need for evangelicalism to embrace the life of the mind. The practical emphasis on worldview and the spiritual life is a central strength of her book.

R. Albert Mohler Jr., J. P. Moreland, Kevin J. Vanhoozer and Andreas J. Kostenberger. *Whatever Happened to Truth?* (Wheaton, Illinois: Crossway, 2005).

Alister E. McGrath. *A Passion for Truth: The Intellectual Coherence of Evangelicalism* (Nottingham, UK: IVP, 1996; Downers Grove, Illinois: IVP, 1999).

D. Michael Lindsay. *Faith in the Halls of Power: How Evangelicals Joined the American Elite* (Oxford: Oxford University Press, 2008).

Charles Colson. *God & Government* (Grand Rapids, Michigan: Zondervan, 2007).

Jim Wallis and Bill Moyers. *Faith Works: How Faith-Based Organizations are Changing Lives, Neighborhoods and America* (Maryknoll, New York: Orbis Books, 1991, 2001).

Albert Mohler asks 'What is truth, and what makes me feel good?' His chapter is one of four in a book with three other excellent treatments of truth. Distinctive evangelical viewpoints on dealing with truth as part of worldview are found in the works of Alister McGrath, Michael Lindsay, Charles Colson, and Jim Wallis. These works show the range of discussion on the topic among evangelicals.

THE CAPE TOWN CALL TO ACTION

UNIT 8

Part 2 • Section IIB-1
Reconciliation

John Paul Lederach. *The Moral Imagination: The Art and Soul of Building Peace* (Oxford: Oxford University Press, 2005).

The author argues for four foundational pillars for lasting reconciliation. 1) The capacity to participate in a nexus of relationships that includes enemies; 2) the ability to learn about differences in other cultures and ethnic groups while suspending value judgment; 3) the belief that reconciliation requires creativity; and 4) the acceptance of the risk associated with change and the unknown (page 5). Lederach ascribes 'moral imagination' to those who possess these traits. The book is for humanitarian workers and project practitioners. Those studying or working in cultures with histories of conflict will find it useful.

Firoza Manji and Patrick Burnett. *African Voices on Development and Social Justice: Editorials from Pambazuka News* (Dar es Salaam: Mkuki Na Nyota Publishers, 2005).

A series of editorials that address contemporary African conflicts, for example the effects of colonialism, the slow process of economic development, and the Rwandan genocide. Each article provides a useful case study to introduce readers to the practical effects of racial conflict. The collection expects a general audience.

Yaacov Bar-Siman-Tov (ed). *From Conflict Resolution to Reconciliation* (Oxford: Oxford University Press, 2004).

This anthology addresses the nebulous concept of reconciliation and seeks to bring clarity to it. Conflict resolution in itself does not lead to lasting peace. Those who wish for peace must pursue something deeper than ceasefire; they must pursue reconciliation. The articles describe the differing results of conflict resolution and reconciliation; the differences between reconciliation among individuals and among groups; the costs and benefits (both perceived and actual) for all parties involved; and mechanisms to achieve reconciliation.

Ian McIntosh. *Aboriginal Reconciliation and the Dreaming: Warramiri Yolngu and the Quest for Equality.* Cultural Survival Studies in Ethnicity and Change (Boston: Allyn and Bacon, 2000).

McIntosh surveys the history of Australian reconciliation attempts, documenting success and failures, past and present. The author then examines aboriginal perspectives on reconciliation and the difficulties the native people face. Students wishing to understand the complexities of indigenous cultures and their relation to other ethnic groups should find this book useful.

Part 2 • Section IIB-1a
Reconciliation, Peace and Jewish Evangelism

Tuvya Zaretsky (ed). *Jewish Evangelism: A Call to the Church.* Occasional Paper No. 60 (Lausanne Committee for World Evangelization, 2005). The 82-page booklet is available for free for download in .pdf at http://www.lausanne.org/docs/2004forum/LOP60_IG31.pdf or at http://www.lausanne.org/en/documents/lops.html

MISHKAN: A Forum on the Gospel and the Jewish People (Pasche Institute of Jewish Studies-A Ministry of Criswell College). Subscription Service, Back issues for publication and authors and subjects are available at http://www.mishkanstore.org

LCJE BULLETIN (A quarterly publication of the Lausanne Consultation on Jewish Evangelism). LCJE membership and *LCJE BULLETIN* subscriptions are available at http://www.lcje.net/Bulletin.html. Current and back issues are available.

All offer a comprehensive introduction to current and historic issues in Jewish evangelism, with bibliographic resources compiled by practitioners. Jewish people internationally have been regarded as unreached and gospel-resistant. Nevertheless, significant missiological work has been done to successfully make the gospel available where the hearts of Jewish people are open and ready to the Spirit of God. Lausanne Occasional Paper #60 was developed by a team of Jewish mission practitioners as a working group at the 2004 Lausanne Forum in Thailand. It introduces the reader to the necessity of Jewish evangelism, the normalcy of Jewish community resistance to discipleship and the relationship between Jewish believers and the Church. *MISHKAN* and the *LCJE BULLETIN* are unique resources for missiological, theological, historical, biblical and apologetic materials for pastors, mission workers and ordinary Christians who want a better understanding of Jewish evangelism.

Yaakov Ariel. *Evangelizing the Chosen People: Missions to the Jews in America, 1880-2000* (Chapel Hill: University of North Carolina, 2000).

Stan Telchin. *Betrayed* (Grand Rapids: Chosen Books, 1986).

Matt Sieger (ed). *Stories of Jews for Jesus* (San Francisco: Purple Pomegranate Productions, 2010).

It is helpful to hear the stories from unreached people who have come to faith in Messiah Jesus. They can offer an emic perspective on the presentation of the gospel. These three resources are for that purpose. Yaakov Ariel is an instructor of Religious Studies at the University of North Carolina at Chapel Hill. He is not a follower of Jesus. However, he has provided an unusually candid and relatively fair assessment of Jewish evangelism efforts, particularly in North America. Christians can learn much from his assessment, criticism of and respect for efforts to communicate Israel's Messiah to her own people. Telchin's story describes his journey as a successful businessman and Jewish community leader who reluctantly yet fervently came to faith in Jesus. Matt Sieger compiled the stories of 19 Jewish people from a variety of professional and social backgrounds, diverse cultural and national citizenships to be joined ultimately by common faith in the Messiah Jesus.

Michael L. Brown. *Answering Jewish Objections to Jesus: General and Historical Objections* (Grand Rapids: Baker Books, 2000). Four additional volumes in the series are also published and available.

David Parker (ed). *Jesus, Salvation and the Jewish People* (London: Paternoster, 2011).

Real Messiah.com a website devoted to answering questions and objections from Jewish people about the Messianic credentials of Jesus. See http://www.therealmessiah.com

> Several excellent resources are available to answer Jewish objections and offer apologetics in the field of Jewish evangelism. Michael L. Brown is a Jewish believer who earned a Ph.D. in Near Eastern Languages and Literature from New York University. His website, apologetic books and frequent debates with rabbis featured on YouTube are tremendous for pastors, academics and Christians engaged in providing Jewish people with answers to common and difficult questions about Jesus.

> David Parker edited papers from a conference sponsored by the World Evangelical Alliance Theological Commission, held in Berlin, Germany, in 2008. The papers offer hope to Europeans and other who wish to present the gospel to Jewish people in the shadow of the Holocaust. The uniqueness of Christ for salvation is the watershed upon which they are asked to stand. It built upon the earlier Willowbank Consultation on the Christian Gospel and the Jewish People held in 1989. That declaration is available at http://www.lcje.net/willowbank.html

Louis Goldberg. *Our Jewish Friends, Revised Edition* (Neptune: Loizeaux, 1983).

Moishe Rosen. *Witnessing to Jews* (San Francisco: Purple Pomegranate Productions, 1998).

Oskar Skarsaune. *In the Shadow of the Temple: Jewish Influences on Early Christianity* (Downers Grove: IVP, 2002).

> Louis Goldberg trained generations of missionary candidates as Professor of Jewish Studies at Moody Bible Institute. Moishe Rosen was the most innovative Jewish mission leader of his generation. Yaakov Ariel, a non-Christian Jewish scholar, credited Rosen with 'Using new strategies and means that made the mission more effective in achieving its goals.' Both writers introduce Christians to some of the basic distinctions of Jewish people and Jewish cultures in North America. Oskar Skarsuane's contribution is part of a much larger project to write the history of the Messianic Jewish movement. It is valuable to the Christian reader for an historically accurate presentation of the Jewish people at the time when the Christian movement began.

Darrell L. Bock and Mitch Glaser (eds). *To the Jew First: The Case for Jewish Evangelism in Scripture and History* (Grand Rapids: Kregel, 2008).

> This collection of fourteen essays covers the issue of the importance of Jewish evangelism from the standpoint of Scripture, theology and mission. It covers an array of topics including Romans 1:16, Romans 9-11, the book of Acts, the message of the prophets and the issue of a future for Israel in God's program.

Mitch Glaser. *Isaiah 53 Explained* (New York: Chosen People Productions, 2010).

> This popular book works through the importance of Isaiah 53 for Jewish missions and is a practical discussion of how to share with the array of Jewish people one meets. It includes a section on common objections one meets in discussing this key text.

Darrell L. Bock and Mitch Glaser (eds). *The Gospel according to Isaiah 53: Encountering the Suffering Servant in Jewish and Christian Theology* (Grand Rapids: Kregel, 2012).

> This work is a more academic discussion of the interpretation of Isaiah 53 in Christian and Jewish sources. It also has practical advice on how to discuss the chapter as well as some sample sermons.

Video: Day of Discovery. *The Mysterious Prophecy of Isaiah 53* (2012).

> This four part series presents online a discussion of Isaiah 53. The show can be seen at http://www.dayofdiscovery.org. This website is full of topics related to Christianity, the gospel, and issues of biblical study and mission.

Other video resources can be found through contacting Jews for Jesus (http://www.jewsforjesus.org) or Chosen People Ministries (http://www.chosenpeople.com) at their respective websites.

PART 2 • SECTION IIB-2
Ethnic Conflict

Joseph Rudolph. *Politics and Ethnicity: A Comparative Study*. Perspectives in Comparative Politics (New York, Macmillan, 2006).

Tracy Robinson-Wood. *The Convergence of Race, Ethnicity, and Gender: Multiple Identities in Counseling*. 4th ed (Upper Saddle River, NJ: Pearson Custom Publishing, 2012).

Joane Nagel. *Race, Ethnicity and Sexuality, Forbidden Frontiers* (Oxford: Oxford University Press, 2003).

Steve Fenton. *Ethnicity (Key Concepts)* (Cambridge: Polity, 2010).

In gathering the following bibliography: (i) we have included books which we realize are not available everywhere in the world; however (ii) we have not listed works which would be available only in libraries.

In selecting books to serve the theological and missiological interest of Lausanne, we have made the following assumptions about the selection as a whole: (i) it should reflect the breadth of literature, while providing a simple framework; (ii) it must be grounded in practical realities faced globally, not just reflect the interests of one part of the world; (iii) all books should start with, or interact with, a biblical or theological base; (iii) the selection needs to help us think more clearly, by reframing questions in new ways, so we do not get stuck with the same answers, where they prove inadequate.

The field of Ethnicity is approached differently by different academic disciplines. For example, in *Politics and Ethnicity*, Joseph Rudolph looks at ethnicity from a political perspective and creates a two-fold classification of ethnic groups depending upon whether a person lives inside or outside their ethnic homeland. He drills down into France, Czechoslovakia, and Nigeria.

Tracy Robinson-Wood in *The Convergence of Race, Ethnicity, and Gender* uses a counseling lens to view ethnicity but separates ethnicity from race and gender. Using the same themes, *Race, Ethnicity and Sexuality, Forbidden Frontiers* by Joane Nagel focuses on justice. Justice has global applications and yet this book is written from a North American context. Robinson-Wood's book does not try to cross international boundaries.

So while some in a counseling setting would separate ethnicity from similar themes, the widely written sociologist Steve Fenton writes in the introduction to his book, *Ethnicity*, that he 'rejects all separation of 'ethnicity' or 'racism' or 'national identity' for the social and theoretical mainstream. It is to re-position the interest in ethnicity within the central domain of the sociological imagination—the structuring of the modern world class formations and class cultures, and the tensions between private lives, cultures and the cohesion of communal and public life.

D. Gellner, J. Pfaff-Czarnecka and J. Whelpton (eds). *Nationalism and Ethnicity in a Hindu Kingdom: The Politics and Culture of Contemporary Nepal*. Studies in Anthropology and History (Overseas Publishers Association, Amsterdam, 1997).

Perhaps ethnic studies are best defined and described by social anthropologists. Traditionally two views have been suggested, a 'primordial view' and a modernist view. According to the first view, writes Gellner in his introduction, 'ethnic (and potentially national) identity has always been a part of social identity'. But the second view 'instrumentalism [modernism] asserts that considerations of political or economic advantage offer the best grounding for the explanation of the success or failure of ethnic movements.' This volume is a great example of deep social anthropology applied in one Asian context.

But none of these seek to develop biblical, theological, or missiological foundations, answers or guidelines for the issues of modern ethnicity. Two books stand out as core foundations to address these needs:

Rogers Brubaker. *Ethnicity without Groups* (Cambridge, MA: Harvard University Press, 2006).

Brubaker, a sociologist, regards ethnicity as a construct, created in the heart and mind of people; he addresses how it is created and what processes affect it. While not theology, this makes us think more deeply about the bricks of division, and how they might instead be used to build a new unity, if Christ has torn down the dividing wall.

Miroslav Volf. *Exclusion and Embrace* (Nashville, Abingdon Press, 1996).

In its entirety, this book deals with ethnicity from the perspective of identity, and how we do/do not and should respond in Christ. This seminal treatise is a must-read for rethinking both the problems that ethnicity creates, and how we as a Christian community usually go about attempting to resolve or ignore those problems.

John Piper. *Bloodlines: Race, Cross, and the Christian* (Wheaton, Illinois, Crossway, 2011).

Piper, grounded in a very American racial interpretation of ethnicity, lays out both biblical and missiological principles. He grapples with questions raised by social anthropologists and counselors.

PART 2 • SECTION IIB-3
Slavery and Human Trafficking

Milton Meltzer. *Slavery: A World History* (New York: Da Capo Press, 1993).

Beginning with the origins of civilization and transition from hunter-gatherers to gardening settlers, Meltzer presents a readable tour of slavery throughout history. He describes various forms, rules, and uses of slavery in different contexts and eras such as Old Testament guidance for treatment of slaves, Roman empire methods of acquiring and releasing slaves, Phoenician kidnappings, historical north African slave trading routes, and the more recent transatlantic slave trade. In illustrating slavery through the ages, Meltzer presents a compelling illustration of the differences – and similarities – between contemporary and historical slavery.

John Wesley. *Thoughts Upon Slavery* (Public Domain, 1774). Available at new.gbgm-umc.org/umhistory/wesley/slavery

John Wesley's 1774 passionate abolitionist pamphlet resonates with the current call to justice in the face of modern day slavery. After a brief but graphic description of the transatlantic slave trade and the people enslaved, Wesley rebuts contemporary justifications and excuses for use of slaves and slave-made goods. As if to the 21st century consumer, he says: 'Indeed you say, 'I pay honestly for my goods; and I am not concerned to know how they are come by.' Nay but you are… Otherwise you are a partaker with a thief, and are not a jot honester than him.' Wesley's indignation at the violent use of human beings as chattel will strike a universal chord with modern-day abolitionists who ask, 'Did the Creator intend that the noblest creatures in the visible world should live such a life as this?'

Kevin Bales. *Disposable People* (Berkeley: University of California Press, 2004).

The first comprehensive description of modern day slavery in its primary forms: labor, sexual servitude, and domestic servitude. Covering both cross-border and domestic slave-trading (*ie* human trafficking), Dr. Bales explains modern incarnations of slavery in its brutality, complexity and human cost.

Hands That Heal: International Curriculum to Train Caregivers of Trafficking Survivors (Academic and Community Based Editions), Faith Alliance Against Slavery and Trafficking (2008).

Kevin Bales. *Ending Slavery* (Berkeley: University of California Press, 2008).

Two resources to guide the reader to abolitionist action: *Hands That Heal* is a comprehensive curriculum written from a biblical perspective to train caregivers who are frontline providers of aftercare for women and children trafficked into the commercial sex industry. *Hands That Heal* is also a tool to inform churches, communities, organizations, and individuals around the world, and inspire them to engage in the battle against the injustice of human trafficking. Its aim is to equip them to develop appropriate responses and transformational care to survivors. The curriculum is the result of collaboration among more than 40 academics and field practitioners from diverse backgrounds and organizations. It is currently being translated into several languages and includes both Academic and Community-based editions. From a broader perspective, Dr. Bales' *Ending Slavery* approaches modern-day slavery with practical solutions from government to individual action. Bales describes broad strategies for governments, organizations and consumers to decrease the prevalence of slavery. Students interested in a strategic overview of the battle against slavery, and students willing to derive concrete applications from more general ideas, would be interested in this book.

Gary A. Haugen. *Just Courage: God's Great Expedition for the Restless Christian* (Downers Grove, Illinois: IVP Books, 2008).

Gary Haugen argues that American Christians often miss God's heart for justice. *Just Courage* aims to compel readers towards lives of courage, vision and sacrifice. Through biblical exposition and personal reflection, Haugen challenges readers to action.

United States Department of State. *2011 US State Department Trafficking in Persons Report.* http://www.state.gov/g/tip/rls/tiprpt/2011/

This report evaluates the extent and severity of slavery around the world. The State Department ranks countries (including the USA) in tiers depending on their government's success in dealing with the injustice. This report can effectively guide strategy for dealing with slavery issues around the world as well as provide recommendations not only for governments, but also nonprofits who want to face the problem.

Film: *Fields of Mudan* (2004). Writer/Director Steve Chang, Florida State University Film School and the Center for the Advancement of Human Rights.

The *Fields of Mudan* is a powerful short film that depicts the story of a young 'Asian' girl and her introduction to life at a brothel. Not more than 6 years old, Mudan, dreams of her mother rescuing her in order to survive the abuse she suffers at the hands of the brothel clients. The film is helpful in understanding modern day slavery in the brothel context in South East Asia.

Film: *Very Young Girls* (2007) documentary film, Director & Producer David Schisgall
http://www.gems-girls.org/get-involved/very-young-girls

Very Young Girls is a documentary that examines the issue of prostitution from the angle of pimps, the girls, law enforcement and courts, the 'johns' that buy sex and a non-profit that provides shelter for formally exploited girls. An expose on commercial sexual exploitation in New York City, *Very Young Girls* enlightens the audience on the complex experience that young girls, often from broken backgrounds confront as their exploiters become 'father figures' to them making it difficult for them to leave the life of prostitution if the opportunity arises. The film depicts the reality of prostitution in the United States, where the average age of the girls entering prostitution is 13.

Film: *Sex+Money: A National Search for Human Worth* (2011) Director Morgan Perry
http://sexandmoneyfilm.com/

Sex+Money: A National Search for Human Worth depicts modern-day slavery and the abolitionist movement in the United States showing the insidious impact on society and the way it manifests itself. Through in-depth interviews from actors engaging the problem from different perspectives, the film informs the audience of the tragedy of modern-day slavery inviting them to join in the fight against it.

PART 2 • SECTION IIB-3
Poverty

William Wilberforce. *A Practical View of Christianity* (Peabody, Mass: Hendrickson Publishers, 1996).

Wilberforce, an 18th century British parliamentarian responsible for abolishing the British slave trade, attempts to reform his readers' understanding of Christianity through introducing them to issues typically ignored from the pulpit. Wilberforce promotes service, justice, and humility as defining characteristics of the Christian faith and argues that those qualities are not present in his contemporary churches. Wilberforce's book is paraphrased by Bob Beltz in *Real Christianity* (Ventura, Calf: Regal Books, 2006).

Martin Luther King Jr. *Letter from the Birmingham Jail* (New York: Limited Editions Club, 2007).

American activist and pastor Martin Luther King Jr. writes to local pastors in response to criticisms. He asks the recipients of his letter to consider the morality of protesting and demonstrations, as well as the morality of silence and complacency. Students engaging justice issues where the governmental authorities support injustice will relate to this work the most.

Henry David Thoreau. *On the Duty of Civil Disobedience* (New Haven: Carl & Margaret Rollins, 1928).

American philosopher Henry David Thoreau writes on American slavery and oppression. Those interested in political philosophy and general treatises on human rights will find this book compelling.

Tom Bingham. *The Rule of Law* (London: Penguin Global, 2010).

Bingham, once the senior law lord of the UK, introduces his readers to the concept of the rule of law- that is, the degree to which law reigns as chief authority in a society. Rule of law secures just treatment for all members of a society while a lack of it provides breeding grounds for injustice. Students wishing to obtain a more theoretical or conceptual grasp of root causes of inequality and injustice can use this book as an introduction.

Thomas Carothers (ed). *Promoting the Rule of Law Abroad: In Search of Knowledge* (Washington, DC: Carnegie Endowment for International Peace, 2006).

Carothers evaluates attempts at legal reform throughout the world first by analyzing such reform conceptually and then by presenting various case studies. This book educates students in systemic problems of justice systems that create room for inequality and injustice. The book also provides illustrations of methods to reform broken justice systems.

Bryant L. Myers. *Walking with the Poor: Principles and Practices of Transformational Development*. Rev. and updated ed (Maryknoll, New York: Orbis Books, 2011).

Myers, currently a professor at Fuller Theological Seminary and a 30 year veteran of the Christian relief and development agency World Vision, presents a practical theory of humanitarian aid. He applies sociological understanding of the root causes of poverty, along with his Christian worldview, to develop his methodology. This work, from an author and organization thoroughly experienced in aid from a Christian standpoint, presents a more practical and less theoretical strategy for serving the poor.

Steve Corbett. *When Helping Hurts: How to Alleviate Poverty Without Hurting the Poor—and Yourself* (Chicago, Illinois: Moody Publishers, 2009).

Corbett and Fikkert first address what they deem to be dysfunctional Christian worldviews. The authors elucidate the complexity of aid work and explain beneficial actions that empower the poor contrasted to well-intentioned but ultimately harmful aid methods. The authors end each chapter with discussion questions, lending utility to individuals or groups of Christians learning to help the underprivileged

Susan R. Holman. *God Knows There's Need: Christian Responses to Poverty* (Oxford: Oxford University Press, 2009).

Susan Holman calls Christians to serve the underprivileged through exposition of early church sources. She then applies early Christian approaches and examples to social engagement to the modern era. Her work should interest any Christian looking for a primer on Christianity and social concerns but especially those with an appreciation for the experiences of the early church.

Jonathan J. Bonk. *Missions and Money*, 2nd edition (Maryknoll, New York: Orbis, 2006).

Bonk's book is not strictly about poverty and oppression, but develops the problem of Western affluence as a missionary problem in a world of poverty and need. The Second Edition adds significant new material on 'the righteous rich' and is a helpful balance to Bonk's earlier edition, which tended to expose the problem while offering fewer constructive solutions. Bonk's study is important reading for Westerners engaged in the missions who often are blind to the problems their affluence can create. This work should be balanced by Corbett and Blomberg.

Paul Collier. *The Bottom Billion: Why the Poorest Countries Are Failing and What Can Be Done About It* (Oxford: Oxford University Press, 2008).

Amartya Sen. *Development As Freedom* (New York: Anchor Books, 1999).

Collier and Sen provide insightful analysis regarding global poverty, as two of the foremost thinkers on the subject. Both write to popular audiences and thus prove to be highly readable. (However those not familiar with economic jargon will still need to wade through some nebulous terrain.) What makes these books noteworthy is the fact that they eschew reductionistic thinking on the topic of poverty, resisting efforts to look at the subject merely by means of economic indicators. Collier explores four 'traps' that countries representing the poorest of the poor (the bottom billion) face: conflict, natural resources, landlocked with bad neighbors, and bad governance; while Sen investigates the way that poverty results from 'unfreedoms', inclusive of social restrictions, injustice, diminished agency, and other limitations. Hence, for both authors, global poverty requires a multifaceted approach that takes economics, social, environmental, and political factors seriously.

Craig L. Blomberg. *Neither Poverty nor Riches: A Biblical Theology of Material Possessions* (Grand Rapids, Michigan: Eerdmans, 1999).

Ronald Sider. *Rich Christians in an Age of Hunger: Moving from Affluence to Generosity* (Nashville: Thomas Nelson, 2005).

Taken together, these books seek to reframe Christian perspectives upon wealth, money, and the poor. Both authors begin with biblical analysis, Blomberg more thoroughly as a biblical scholar. Sider engages Scripture on the topic of poverty in order to speak prophetically into contemporary contexts. Balanced, thorough, contemporary and comprehensively biblical, Blomberg's book may be the best biblical theology on wealth and poverty. The summary chapter is an outstanding overview of the Bible's teaching on how believers should view their money and possessions. Both contend with materialism, especially such varieties as make their way into Western Christianity. The Sider book engages the political leanings of Christians, whether to the right (conservatives) or left (liberals), that tend to distort the real essence of wealth. He concludes with tangible solutions that everyday Christians might do to more faithfully represent Christ in their world.

Yale University, Faith and Globalization Initiative. In partnership with Tony Blair Faith Foundation. http://faithandglobalization.yale.edu/

This website offer a wonderful repository of resources for tackling the complex, interdisciplinary issues associated with globalization. Yale University, in partnership with the Tony Blair Foundation, offers free videos (downloadable or streaming), as well as a host of other resources dealing with intersections of faith and globalization. Those interested in poverty do not need to look far. On the website, one can find lectures by esteemed scholars such as Miroslav Volf, Nicholas Wolterstorff, and Douglas Rae that grapple with issues of politics, poverty reduction, environmental decay, public health, and human rights.

David S. Landes. *The Wealth and Poverty of Nations* (New York/London: W. W. Norton & Company, 1999).

Landes asks the question, 'Why do some nations achieve economic success while others languish in poverty?' To answer such an audacious query, he traces the historical contours of the dilemma, proving that there is no easy answer to this quandary but rather rich interplay of historical, cultural, and environmental factors. The historian reminds us that if we are going to help solve this issue for future generations, we would be wise to learn from the past.

Bryant L. Myers. *Working with the Poor* (Maryknoll, New York: Orbis, 2008).

How do Christian practitioners express authentically holistic transformational development? This is the challenge to World Vision development practitioners and to all non-government organizations concerned about community development that addresses the whole person and the entire community. This dilemma is rooted in the western assumption that the physical and spiritual realms are separate and distinct from one another. Such a dichotomy leads to a belief among practitioners that restoring people's relationship with God has nothing to do with restoring just political, social and economic relationships among people. Even Christians often believe God's redemptive work takes place in the spiritual realm, while the world is seemingly left to the devil.

But the Bible never separates the physical from the spiritual - the rule of God permeates both. In this volume, development practitioners struggle to overcome the problem of dualism and find a way toward a more genuinely holistic approach to helping the poor. Experienced development practitioners reflect on: Understanding poverty, Participatory learning and action, Appreciative inquiry, The Bible and transformational development, Sustainable economic development, Community transformation in the urban context, Community development and peacebuilding.

Everyone wanting to engage in transformational development will find new insights and essential learnings from these hands-on practitioners.

Bryant L. Myers. *Walking with the Poor* (Maryknoll, New York: Orbis, 2011).

In this revised and updated edition of a modern classic, Bryant Myers shows how Christian mission can contribute to dismantling poverty and social evil. Integrating the best principles and practice of the international development community, the thinking and experience of Christian nongovernmental organizations (NGOs), and a theological framework for transformational development, Myers demonstrates what is possible when we cease to treat the spiritual and physical domains of life as separate and unrelated.

Brian Fikkert and Steve Corbett. *When Helping Hurts: Alleviating Poverty Without Hurting the Poor…and Yourself* (Chicago: Moody Press, 2009).

When Helping Hurts combines sound theology, solid research, foundational principles, and proven strategies that prepare you for Christian transformational ministry among the poor, whether in the local community or abroad. Good intentions are not enough. Churches and individual Christians can have faulty assumptions about the causes of poverty, which lead to ministry strategies which do considerable harm to poor people as well as to themselves. *When Helping Hurts* addresses these assumptions and offers principles and strategies for poverty alleviation, including: the distinction between relief, rehabilitation, and development; the difference between asset-based and needs-based strategies; and the advantages of participatory over blueprint approaches.

PART 2 • SECTION IIB-4
People with Disabilities

Romel W. Mackelprang. *Disability: A Diversity Model Approach in Human Service Practice.* 2nd ed (Chicago: Lyceum Books, 2009).

The author provides a guide for those who work with persons of disabilities. The book employs an 'empowerment' method to provide patients with better independence.

Paul K. Longmore. *Why I Burned My Book and Other Essays on Disability. American subjects* (Philadelphia: Temple University Press, 2003).

Joni Eareckson Tada and Nigel M. de S. Cameron. *How to be a Christian in a Brave New World.* Grand Rapids, Zondervan, 2006. Kindle ebook, 2009).

Longmore presents a variety of essays attempting to evaluate the social obstacles to persons with disabilities. He writes on bioethics, politics, and the need for activism in the face of systemic prejudice and discrimination towards disabled persons.

Joni Eareckson Tada, a global ambassador for people with disabilities, joins Nigel Cameron, bio-ethicist and theologian, to open up major bio-ethical questions of the bio-tech century. Students exploring the arena of disability will want to engage with the principles expounded in this unique book.

Part 2 • Section IIB-5
HIV/AIDS

The following websites sponsor a wealth of information and are frequently updated. Some link to thousands of free journal abstracts and downloadable articles. Many have current fact sheets on aspects of the epidemic including the disease process, evidence-based interventions, prevention and care, epidemiology, age and gender-specific needs, and regional issues. Others have manuals to assist in strategy development, training, and program implementation.

National Institutes of Health. Washington DC. http://AIDSinfo.nih.gov

United Nations. UNAIDS. Geneva. http://UNAIDS.org (more on this below)

World Bank. Washington DC. http://worldbank.org

World Health Organization. Geneva. http://www.who.int/hiv/

FHI 360 Satellife: Health Information and Technology. Watertown, MA. http://www.healthnet.org

Institute for Development Studies. Sussex, UK. http://www.eldis.org/hivaids/index/htm

Wiley Online Library. http://www.onlinelibrary.wiley.com

Centers for Disease Control and Prevention. Atlanta. http://www.CDC.gov/hiv

International HIV/AIDS Alliance. Hove, UK. http://www.aidsalliance.org

Jamison D.T., Breman J.G., Measham A.R., et al (eds). 'HIV/AIDS Prevention and Treatment,' Chap 18 in *Disease Control Priorities in Developing Countries.* 2nd edition. Washington DC: World Bank, 2006. Available at http://www.ncbi.nlm.nih.gov/books/NBK11782

Kenneth Mayer and H.F. Pizer (eds). *The AIDS Pandemic: Impact on Science and Society* (San Diego: Elsevier Academic Press, 2005).

This classic has contributions from scientists and practitioners connected to major schools of public health in the United States, South Africa, and India. Parts of the book are technical covering science and clinical aspects of care. The chapters 'AIDS Behavioral Prevention: Unprecedented Progress and Emerging Challenges,' 'The Ever-changing Face of AIDS' are must-reads. Lessons learned from the economic implications of AIDS, Africa's experience with the crisis, and concerns for human rights in Asia are well described.

United Nations. *Global Report: UNAIDS Report on the Global Epidemic 2010.* http://www.unaids.org/globalreport/Global_report.htm

This report summarizes the United Nation's evaluation of progress on the Millennium Development Goals. In doing so it presents a thorough analysis of HIV/AIDS infection rates and consequences around the world. The report provides a girth of data—statistics, census counts, maps and graphics—useful to anyone wishing to become acquainted with the global epidemic, learn about worldwide trends, or inform others.

Paul Volberding, Merle Sande, Joep Lange, Warner Green, Joel Gallant. *Global HIV/AIDS Medicine* (Elsevier: New York, USA, 2007).

This is a comprehensive work on the biology and spread of the disease, prevention methods, diagnosis and treatment, prevention and management in high resource regions as well as low resource regions, and the social and economic effects of the epidemic. It serves as a virtual encyclopedia to HIV/AIDS. Students who wish to minister specifically to HIV/AIDS victims will find it valuable.

Emma Guest. *Children of AIDS: Africa's Orphan Crisis.* 2nd ed (London: Pluto Press, 2003).

Guest compiles stories of HIV/AIDS orphans and community servants from Africa. Through emotive stories she introduces readers to one of the devastating effects of HIV/AIDS in Africa. *NB:* With the exception of Chapter 4, Guest does not offer practical solutions or guidance, and does not offer thorough analyses of underlying societal causes. This book attempts to compel students outside of Africa to care for children orphaned by HIV/AIDS.

HIV/AIDS Toolkit: What Your Church Can Do (Lake Forest, CA: Saddleback Resources).
http://www.saddlebackresources.com/HIVAIDS-Toolkit-What-Your-Church-Can-Do-2Audio-CDs1DVD1Resource-Materials-CD-P2893.aspx

This kit aims to be a complete resource in one package. It includes sample sermons, strategies for beginning HIV/AIDS ministries in a church, and multimedia tools to engage congregations. Ministry practitioners in developed nations can apply these resources to reach out to those affected by HIV/AIDS.

Edward Green. *Rethinking AIDS Prevention: Learning from Successes in Developing Countries* (Westport, Connecticut: Praeger, 2003).

Edward Green presents compelling evidence that the turnaround in Uganda's frightening trajectory of new HIV infections in the 1990s was largely due to a multifaceted approach in HIV prevention that included a strong emphasis on abstinence before marriage and 'zero grazing' or faithfulness in marriage.

Edward Green and Allison Ruark. AIDS, Behavior, and Culture (Walnut Creek, California: Left Coast Press, 2011).

Maintaining his theme of prevention that is comprehensive and largely behavior-driven, this book explores the critical importance of tailoring strategies to local culture and avoiding a western-imposed approaches to HIV prevention.

World Relief. Families for Life. Baltimore and Chennai, India, 2012.

This interactive series designed to help strengthen marriages as a means of HIV prevention was developed in India for local churches and draws principles for marriage from Song of Solomon with four basic themes: friends for life, attracted for life, fulfilled for life, and committed for life. Available for download from World Relief.
http://www.worldrelief.org

TEARFUND, Kidsalive International, Kindernot Hilfe, World Relief, Norwegian Church AID, World Vision, MAP International, Viva Network, Compassion, Moravian Church, ARCA Associates. *Let Your Light Shine: Caring for Children Affected by HIV.* 2008

This curriculum toolkit includes 12 video modules, two documentaries on DVD, an electronic form as well as hard copies of a User's Guide and Facilitator's Book. There are twelve modules that are geared toward helping children affected and/or infected with HIV and include topics such as 'The Healthy African Child', 'Children and HIV: 0-5 Years', 'Children and HIV: 6-12 Years', and 'Caring for the Caregiver.' Available through any of the organizations listed.

Global Network of People Living with HIV and AIDS. http://www.gnpplus.net

Strategies for Hope. http://www.stratshope.org

This website has free downloads of their popular series of booklets on community and church-based interventions in HIV/AIDS in Africa. The newest series, 'Called to Care Toolkit', offers specific help for persons and families living with HIV and covers issues on pastoral and community support, trauma, parents, nutrition, and communication. The booklets are sprinkled with case studies and are designed for community and church level programs. The series is available in English, Portuguese, French, and Kiswahili.

Faith to Action Initiative. http://www.faithbasedcarefororphans.org

The above (i) report on research relating to the care of children orphaned by AIDS and (ii) advocate strongly for children to be supported through families not orphanages. Two companion publications, *From Faith to Action* and *Journeys of Faith* may be downloaded for information and study with church groups.

Geoff Foster, Carol Levine, John Williamson. *A Generation At Risk: The Global Impact of HIV/AIDS on Orphans and Vulnerable Children* (Cambridge: Cambridge University Press, 2005).

Joint Learning Initiative on Children and HIV/AIDS. http://www.JLICA.org

Geoff Foster, Linda Richter, Lorraine Sherr. *Where the Heart Is: Meeting the Psychosocial Needs of Young Children in the Context of HIV/AIDS* (Bernard van Leer Foundation, the Netherlands, 2006).

Patrick Dixon. *The Truth About AIDS—and a Practical Christian Response*, 4th ed (London: ACET Alliance and Operation Mobilization, 2004).

Patrick Dixon, founder of AIDS Care, Education, and Training (ACET), an international alliance based in the UK, has been an early advocate for a Christian response to AIDS. This work, a fourth edition, provides a comprehensive review of timeless issues surrounding AIDS and includes an extensive appendix with practical helps in areas such as caregiver training, orphan support, a basic training manual on HIV/AIDS, and economic development.

Ezra Chitando (ed). *Mainstreaming HIV and AIDS in Theological Education* (Geneva: WCC Publications, 2008).

This scholarly piece has a distinct advantage of African theologians and HIV/AIDS experts speaking directly to this critical concern on the continent. Perspectives from many African countries, churches, and communities are voiced. NB: Included is a comprehensive bibliography of published and unpublished papers relating to the church and HIV/AIDS.

Micah Network. *A Christian Response to HIV and AIDS*. http://www.micahnetwork.org

Tearfund. 'HIV and AIDS: Taking Action'. *Roots*.
http://www.tilz.tearfund.org/webdocs/Tilz/Roots/English/HIVandAIDS

Intended to download, the chapter from Tearfund is comprehensive, interactive, and church-focused with Scriptural foundations for major themes including prevention, care, and orphan support. If a local church or development group could access only one source, this would be the 'one-stop' piece that would take them far in developing an effective program.

Deborah Dortzbach and Meredith Long. *The AIDS Crisis: What We Can Do* (Downers Grove: IVP, 2006).

The AIDS crisis is an opportunity for God's people to be a sanctuary of care, hope, guidance, and compassion and this book illustrates the many ways in which the church across the world is engaged. Critical issues swirling around the crisis are reflectively addressed including sexuality, stigma, prevention, orphan care, judgment and grace, gender, power, and culture. While this book needs updating in technical areas of current practice in HIV prevention, epidemiology, and the science of HIV, the core biblical themes of sexuality and the Christian's response to care are timeless.

World Relief. *Our Communities: A Pastoral Counseling Manual for AIDS*, 2005.

Developed after years of pastoral counseling workshops in Africa and Asia, this manual is a step-by-step curriculum to train pastors and lay leaders in the goals of pastoral counseling, counseling skill development, and the biblical basis for counseling situations. Teaching case studies are used for hands-on practice sessions. Contact World Relief for downloading the manual. http://www.worldrelief.org

World Relief. *Choose Life: Guide for Peer Educators and Youth Leaders*, 2005.

A series of two manuals, one for ages 10-14 years and one for ages 15 years and older, this series has been widely used in schools, communities, and churches throughout Africa and parts of Asia. The manuals were based on behavior change and adult education principles and are interactive, and provide specific instruction for peer educators that help youth work through significant life issues relating to abstinence before marriage and faithfulness in marriage.

PART 2 • SECTION IIB-6
Stewardship and Creation

Ed Brown. *Our Father's World: Mobilizing the Church to Care for Creation* (Downers Grove: IVP, 2008).

Our Father's World is particularly suited for seminarians headed for pastoral ministry. The first half of the book develops a number of theological themes (God as creator; effects of the fall; the role of the church in responding to environmental challenges) that are similar to those found in other books in this list. The unique benefit of *Our Father's World* will be found in application chapters that focus on church ministry: Worship, children's programming, buildings and grounds – and even evangelism. Brown is the founding director of Care of Creation Inc., and a former pastor and missionary. The book is not highly academic, but is useful because of its practical congregational focus.

Peter Harris. *Kingfisher's Fire: A Story of Hope for God's Earth* (Oxford: Monarch Books, 2008).

Peter Harris' book shares inspiring stories of communities engaged in creation care throughout the world. The book is based on the work of A Rocha, an international Christian conservation organization that Peter and his wife Miranda founded, which is active in over twenty countries on five continents. This is an accessible and important read for anyone working across cultures in both rural and urban contexts.

J. Matthew Sleeth. *Serve God Save the Planet: A Christian Call to Action* (Grand Rapids: Zondervan, 2007).

Matthew Sleeth was a very successful medical doctor when he came to faith in Christ and discovered a calling to care for creation and encourage others to do so as well. This book—based on the faith and environmental journey of Sleeth and his family—is a good entry point to start thinking about creation care from a very personal and practical perspective. It is very readable and engaging book that has made a great impact in many lives and churches across the United States.

Ben Lowe. *Green Revolution: Coming Together to Care for Creation* (Downers Grove: IVP, 2009).

Green Revolution is a creation care manifesto written from the perspective of the generation next in line to inherit God's earth: the Millennials. Drawing from the international experiences of the author and stories from campuses and churches around North America, it calls the church to take the next step beyond individual action, and work together to affect change on a larger scale. This book is a key resource in understanding the creation care movement that is renewing our biblical discipleship and Christian witness.

Fred Van Dyke. *Between Heaven and Earth: Christian Perspectives on Environmental Protection* (Santa Barbara: Praeger, 2010).

Noah Toly and Daniel Block (eds). *Keeping God's Earth: The Global Environment in Biblical Perspective* (Downers Grove: IVP, 2010).

These two books are written at the academic level and both make critical contributions to creation care knowledge and practice. *Between Heaven and Earth* lays out a thorough and insightful analysis of Christian environmental ethics, biblical foundations, and historical postures and practices of the church. It goes a step further by casting a bold vision of faithful creation care moving forward. *Keeping God's Earth* is a unique volume that features an expert collection of biblical scholars and scientists who team up to address major theological themes and contemporary issues including the diversity of life, water resources, global climate change, and cities and the environment.

National Association of Evangelicals. *Loving the Least of These: Addressing a Changing Environment* (2011). Booklet available for free download at http://www.nae.net/lovingtheleastofthese.

Jim Ball. *Global Warming and the Risen LORD: Christian Discipleship and Climate Change* (Washington, DC: Evangelical Environmental Network, 2010).

These two resources focus in on the growing contemporary challenge of global climate change. Both emphasize the biblical foundation for creation care and the heavily disproportionate impacts that climate change is having and will continue to have on many poor communities and developing nations. Global climate change is one of the leading justice and environmental issues of our time and a reality that the global church is already grappling with. Both publications provide the background understanding and helpful recommendations for churches to be faithful in this area.

Ray C. Anderson. Mid-Course Correction: Toward a Sustainable Enterprise: The Interface Model (Atlanta, Georgia: Peregrinzilla Press, 1998).

Through his own professional story Ray Anderson paints a picture of the practical transition from traditional business practices to sustainable and environmental practice. He also uses his own business to demonstrate practical methods other businesses can employ as well.

International Bulletin of Missionary Research, Vol 35, No 3, July 2011

Most of this issue of the *IBMR* is devoted to 'Mission and the Care of Creation.' Particularly helpful are articles by Dana Robert on 'Historical Trends in Missions and Earth Care' and a case study from Kenya by Craig Sorley. The article by M. L Daneel is less helpful from an evangelical perspective, but the whole issue is worth referencing.

Bill McKibben. *Deep Economy: The Wealth of Communities and the Durable Future*. 1st ed (New York: Times Books, 2007).

McKibben challenges the assumptions that the goal of economics and economy is to produce endless and unlimited economic growth. In light of the earth's limited resources, the author presents various new paradigms that better use natural resources and avert ecological fallout.

Donella H. Meadows. *The Limits to Growth: The 30-Year Update* (White River Junction, Vermont: Chelsea Green Publishing Company, 2004).

An update of a seminal book from the 1970s, Meadows introduces readers to the concept of scarcity of resources on a global scale. She argues that businesses and consumers have consumed more resources and produced more harmful products than the planet's ecosystem can effectively handle. Meadows illustrates tools to transition societies to more responsible consumers of the earth's limited resources.

Ken Gnanakan. *God's World* (International Study Guides series. London: SPCK, 1999).

This study guide combines a discussion of the theology and ethics of the environment with a practical, positive Christian response. It covers themes from both the Old and New Testament and includes detailed discussion of actual passages and the wider issues involved The book presents various case studies on practical approaches to environmental protection.

THE CAPE TOWN CALL TO ACTION

UNIT 9

PART 2 • SECTION IIC-1
People of Other Faiths

This bibliographic section represents a Christian response to the Great Commission, and more specifically focuses on reaching people of other faiths. One of the most important aspects of reaching adherents of other religions is to understand the foundation and basic tenants of the religion itself. The section below, therefore, provides suggestions for resources that can educate the reader in each of these religions, as well as provide preparation for reaching adherents of each religion with the gospel of Jesus Christ.

This first section covers world religions and anthologies.

James A. Beverly. *Religions A to Z: A Guide to the 100 Most Influential Religious Movements* (Nashville: Thomas A. Nelson, 2005).

John L. Brockington. *Hinduism and Christianity* (Hampshire: Macmillan Press, 1992).

Todd M. Johnson, and Kenneth R. Ross (eds). *Atlas of Global Christianity* (Edinburgh: Edinburgh University Press, 2009).

Mark Juergensmeyer (ed). *Global Religions: An Introduction* (Oxford: Oxford University Press, 2003).

Stephen Prothero. *God is Not One: The Eight Rival Religions that Run the World – and Why Their Differences Matter* (New York: HarperCollins, 2010).

Timothy C. Tennent. *Christianity at the Religious Roundtable: Evangelicalism in Conversation with Hinduism, Buddhism, and Islam* (Grand Rapids: Baker Academic, 2002).

The six books listed above offer the reader an opportunity to learn about and compare multiple religions in a single resource. As a shorter version of his larger book, *Nelson's Illustrated Guide to Religions*, Beverly's *Religions A to Z* is comprised of short introductions for 100 world religions. A brief history is given for each, and recommendations for resources for further study are also included. Brockington offers an opportunity for comparison and dialogue, focusing on Hinduism and Christianity. Johnson and Ross's *Atlas of Global Christianity* provides charts, maps, and articles from scholars around the world regarding the statistical progress of global Christianity as well as other religions, uniquely highlighting the contexts of cities, peoples, and languages. Juergensmeyer counters the perception that adherents of the world's religions are clumped together in confined geographic areas, instead highlighting world religions in their contemporary global contexts. Prothero attempts to debunk the theory that all religions are the same by presenting eight contemporary world religions according to the human problem each one addresses and their respective solutions. The reviews of Prothero's book are mixed, but the book does provide an important impetus for dialogue and religious literacy. Tennent expounds and compares the doctrine of God in Christianity with parallel teachings in Hinduism, Buddhism, and Islam. While learning about these religions, the reader also observes a dialogue with adherents of each on a deep, theological level.

The following deal with Hinduism.

Wendy Doniger. *The Hindus: An Alternative History* (New York: Penguin, 2009).

Karma to Grace. Resources available at http://www.karma2grace.org/

Julius Lipner. *Hindus: Their Religious Beliefs and Practices* (London: Routledge, 1994).

Hillary P. Rodrigues. *Introducing Hinduism* (New York: Routledge, 2006).

Ravi Zacharias. *New Birth or Rebirth? Jesus talks with Krishna* (Colorado Springs: Multnomah Books, 2008).

Doniger's book offers an historical account of Hinduism from 50 million BC to the present era. Her recounting of history seamlessly incorporates the ancient Hindu texts, thereby simultaneously educating the reader in both arenas. The website http://www.karma2grace.org is a valuable online resource facilitating the understanding of key concepts in Hinduism and Christianity. It also includes testimonies of people who have come to faith in Christ as their Savior. Lipner provides an accessible, foundational account of the religion of the Hindus. He addresses the multifaceted definitions and themes of Hinduism very well and creatively presents the reader with a solid understanding of the basic tenets of Hinduism and the threads by which they are held together. Rodrigues's book is a newer addition to this area of scholarship and offers a well-organized, thorough, and sensitive overview of Hinduism. It includes a helpful glossary and also includes reference to a companion website. Zacharias's work is a concise, easy-to-read book in which a fictional dialogue between Jesus, Krishna, and a third party educates the reader about both Christianity and Hinduism. It creatively supplies impetus for thought and learning.

The following deal with Buddhism.

William Theodore de Bary (ed). *The Buddhist Tradition in India, China, and Japan* (New York: Random House, Inc., 1972).

Charles S. Prebish and Damien Keown. *Introducing Buddhism* (New York: Routledge, 2006).

David Lin and Steve Spalding (eds). *Sharing Jesus in the Buddhist World* (Pasadena: William Carey Library, 2003).

The slightly older account of Buddhist thought and scriptures in de Bary's work offers the reader an opportunity to learn from the original Buddhist texts and hear directly from Buddhist thinkers. Its inclusion of Buddhist thought from India, China, and Japan give it credibility and thoroughness of presentation. Prebish and Keown provide a thorough overview of Buddhism that includes history, foundations, development, contemporary issues, and more—miraculously, under 300 pages. This helpful resource is an excellent introduction for anyone seeking to better understand Buddhist neighbors and friends. Lin and Spalding's book is a concise and helpful guide to understanding the missiological issues involved in presenting Jesus in Buddhist contexts.

The following deal with Islam.

Abdiyah Akbar Abdul-Haqq. *Sharing Your Faith with a Muslim* (Minneapolis: Bethany House Publishers, 1980).

Kenneth Cragg. *Jesus and the Muslim: An Exploration* (Oxford: Oneworld, 2003).

John L. Esposito. *Islam: The Straight Path*. 3rd Edition (Oxford: Oxford University Press, 1998).

Caesar E. Farah. *Islam*. 6th ed (Hauppauge: Barron's Educational Series, 2000).

Phil Parshall, Phil. *Understanding Muslim Teachings and Traditions: A Guide for Christians* (Grand Rapids: Baker Books, 1994).

J. Dudley Woodbury (ed). *From Seed to Fruit: Global Trends, Fruitful Practices, and Emerging Issues among Muslims* (Pasadena: William Carey Library, 2008).

Parshall, Farah, and Esposito are all helpful resources in understanding Islam. Farah provides a broad scope of the foundation, beliefs, sects, and tenets of Islam while Parshall focuses on specific doctrines and topics such as prayer, hell, Muhammad, and paradise. Esposito's book flows nicely as it discusses the interpretations of foundational principles of Islam and how they are lived out in present societies. Akbar, Craig, and Woodbury all offer perspectives on how to reach Muslims with the gospel of Jesus Christ in today's complex and intricate relational cultures.

The following deal with Judaism.

Yaakov Ariel. *Evangelizing the Chosen People: Missions to the Jews in America, 1880-2000* (Chapel Hill: University of North Carolina Press, 2000).

Moishe Rosen. *Witnessing to Jews: Practical Ways to Relate the Love of Jesus* (San Francisco: Purple Pomegranate Productions, 1998).

Fenton Ward. *What to say when they say I'm Jewish: Sharing the Gospel with the Original Messengers*. 2nd ed (San Francisco: Purple Pomegranate Productions, 1999).

Online resources can also be accessed at http://www.kesherjournal.com

Ariel's book provides a history of the evangelization of Jews in America during a specific time period, discussing both mistakes and successes. If one can learn from history, then this book is one of the most useful resources available. Rosen's book gives the reader information and confidence in understanding the barriers that prevent Jews from receiving Jesus as their Messiah, and gives instruction regarding how to communicate in a way that gently addresses those barriers in order to open a path for communication. Ward's book likewise combines helpful strategies for communicating the Christian faith. He also supplies explanations of key passages from the Bible to help Christians communicate well with their Jewish neighbors and friends. The Kesher Journal in an online resource that mainly houses articles from the Helsinki Consultation on Jewish Continuity in the Body of Messiah but also houses book reviews relevant to their focus.

The following deal with additional religions.

John H. Berthrong and Evelyn Nagai. *Confucianism: A Short Introduction.* Reprint (Oxford: Oneworld Publications, 2004).

Robert Ellwood. *Introducing Japanese Religion* (Abington: Routledge, 2008).

Livia Kohn. *Introducing Daoism* (Abington: Routledge, 2009).

W. H. McLeod. *Exploring Sikhism: Aspects of Sikh Identity, Culture, and Thought* (New Delhi: Oxford University Press, 2000).

Mario Poceski. *Introducing Chinese Religions* (Abington: Routledge, 2009).

Fung Yu-lan. *A Short History of Chinese Philosophy.* Ed Derk Bodde (New York: The Free Press, 1948).

The above texts are helpful and well-written. The Routledge series is especially well written, thorough, and concise.

PART 2 • SECTION IIC-2
Suffering

Michael Budde and Karen Scott (eds). *Witness of the Body: The Past, Present, and Future of Christian Martyrdom* (Grand Rapids, Michigan: Eerdmans, 2011).

In this volume, twelve scholars from across academic disciplines demystify Christian martyrdom and re-situate it within the everyday practices of the church. Beginning with the persecution of early Christians by the Roman Empire, *Witness of the Body* explores the place of martyrdom in the church through all ages and into the future. Part One of the book deals with martyrdom and persecution as a witness of the church; Part Two demonstrated how martyrdom builds the church; Part Three shows how martyrdom can be a destroyer of the church. The last part considers contemporary political situations and the role of Christian martyrdom as a witness of Christ's church in a hostile world.

Keith E. Eitel (ed). *Missions in Contexts of Violence* (Pasadena, California: William Carey Library, 2007).

The writers of this volume deal with doing mission work in the context of violence. They give a list of missionaries and others whose lifestyles, strategies, and practices in specific contexts of violence and gross violation of human rights, provide rich experience of how to tell the gospel story in such inhuman conditions.

Ajith Fernando. *The Call to Joy & Pain: Embracing suffering in Your Ministry* (Nottingham, UK: IVP, 2008; Wheaton, Illinois: Crossway Books, 2008).

The call to suffer is a call to joyful living. Fernando clearly demonstrates that suffering and joy are essential to Christian discipleship and that suffering draws believers closer to Christ and makes the church grow in its commitment to Christ and to the preaching of the gospel.

James and Marti Hefley. *By Their Blood: Christian Martyrs of the Twentieth Century.* 2nd ed (Grand Rapids, Michigan: Baker Books, 1996).

Now thoroughly updated to include martyrs from 1900, the book presents testimonies of the steadfast faith of modern Christians all over the world. The hundreds of stories of devotion will inspire readers to a more fervent faith and an appreciation of the freedom they have in Christ. The Hefleys bring to the attention of the world the sacrifice of many modern Christians who are giving their lives for the gospel. They help contemporary believers to be aware that martyrdom is a current affair and is not relegated solely to the ancient past and must be expected by faithful followers of Christ.

Harold D. Hunter and Cecil M. Robeck, Jr. (eds). *The Suffering Body: Responding to the Persecution of Christians* (Waynesboro, Georgia: Paternoster Press, 2006).

The authors remind readers that suffering with Christ was not only the experience of the early church but of much of the church of twenty-first century also. In addition to presenting the theological foundation of Christian suffering, the book presents up to date, global reflections on the different ways in which the church suffers: from class discrimination to government persecution; from interreligious conflict to tensions between different Christian groups. Different contributors share the Christian suffering and response to suffering from different contexts, namely Africa, the Middle East, Central and Eastern Europe, and Asia.

John Piper and Justin Taylor. *Suffering and the Sovereignty of God* (Wheaton, Illinois: Crossway Books, 2006).

The writers of this book discuss the sovereignty of God, his purpose and his grace in suffering, and tackle some of the hardest and most significant issues of Christian concern. In addition to the biblical and theological framework on the subject of suffering, the book offers pastoral wisdom, theological conviction, biblical insight, and spiritual counsel to those suffering or ministering to a hurting world.

Part 2 • Section IIC-3
Grace

We are the aroma of Christ. Our calling is to live and serve among people of other faiths in a way that is so saturated with the fragrance of God's grace that they smell Christ, that they come to taste and see that God is good. By such embodied love, we are to make the gospel attractive in every cultural and religious setting. When Christians love people of other faiths through lives of love and acts of service, they embody the transforming grace of God. In cultures of 'honour', where shame and vengeance are allied with religious legalism, 'grace' is an alien concept. In these contexts, God's vulnerable, self-sacrificing love is not something to be debated; it is considered too foreign, even repulsive. Here, grace is an acquired taste, over a long time, in small doses, for those hungry enough to dare to taste it. The aroma of Christ gradually permeates all that his followers come into contact with.

Richard J. Mouw. *Uncommon Decency: Christian Civility in an Uncivil World*, 2nd edition (Downers Grove, Illinois: IVP, 2010).

Terry Muck and Frances S. Adeney. *Christianity Encountering World Religions: The Practice of Mission in the Twenty-first Century* (Grand Rapids, Michigan: Baker Academic, 2009).

Mouw introduces the classic problem of conviction without civility. Evangelicals who hold strongly to the uniqueness of Christ and the authority of Scripture need to cultivate a civility built on the grace of God. Mouw explores the issues of living out convicted civility as a way of loving and serving among people of other faiths. Muck and Adeney provide an introduction to the encounter between Christians and people who hold the faith and culture of other religions. They begin by covering the essential perspectives in interfaith life and witness. Muck and Adeney then provide historical examples of sensitive witness and an exploration of a methodology of gracious encounter with people of other faiths. Finally, the authors offer an approach to mission they call 'giftive' mission, building on the biblical metaphor of offering gifts and based solidly on the grace of God.

Evangelical Interfaith Dialogue, A journal for evangelicals involved in interfaith dialogue as committed disciples of Jesus Christ. Journal available for free download at http://evangelicalinterfaithconversation.blogspot.com/

Vinoth Ramachandra. Faiths in Conflict? Christian Integrity in a Multicultural World (Downers Grove, Illinois: IVP, 1999).

John G. Stackhouse, Jr. *Humble Apologetics: Defending the Faith Today* (Oxford: Oxford University Press, 2002).

Timothy C. Tennett. *Christianity at the Religious Roundtable: Evangelicalism in Conversation with Hinduism, Buddhism, and Islam* (Grand Rapids, Michigan: Baker Academic, 2002).

The additional journal and books add depth to the conversation of a gracious approach to people of other religious traditions. Evangelical Interfaith Dialogue explores a range of topics as a journal launched by students committed to Jesus Christ who are seeking to be faithful, gracious witnesses. Approaching the issues from a context of interreligious encounter and strife, Ramachandra challenges the quick responses based on stereotypes while building a case for belief in Christ as an enigma in the religious landscape. Stackhouse takes on the combative witness found in the apologetic tradition based on competing beliefs. He calls for a humble approach to others with vision for helping others toward a health in all aspects of their lives including their relationship to God. Tennett builds on the rich tradition of interfaith dialogue as an approach to sharing our faith in conversation with other faiths. With a deep-seated commitment to the truth of Scripture, Tennett introduces the approach to defending the historic Christian faith based on the relevant texts and traditions of each faith.

PART 2 • SECTION IIC-4
Discipleship

Christopher Adsit. *Personal Disciple Making: A Step by Step Guide for Leading a Christian from New Birth to Maturity* (Nashville: Thomas Nelson Publishers, 1988).

This is a very practical handbook discussing the basics of discipleship. Adsit frames his strategy on moving people through the biblically-defined levels of spiritual maturity: babies, children, adolescents and adults. He then seeks to prescribe the spiritual input each might need. This book has many charts and outlines that could be taken and used directly in a discipleship relationship. Adsit comes from a Campus Crusade background, and advances the *Ten Basic Steps* as suitable tools for training.

George Barna. *Growing True Disciples* (Colorado Springs: Waterbrook, 2001).

Barna bases his study on the case studies of nine contemporary churches which have been highly effective in producing spiritually mature believers. He surveys the approaches used in the various churches, and identifies the 'common denominators' he believes have proven effective. He also includes a section where he details practices which didn't seem to work as well. Barna then proposes a best-practice style model which incorporates different elements of the respective effective discipling ministry from the various churches. This is a helpful description of what is working well in various contexts to produce genuine life change and growth.

Dietrich Bonhoeffer. *The Cost of Discipleship* (New York: Touchstone, 1995).

The Cost of Discipleship, first published in German in 1937, was Bonhoeffer's answer to the questions, 'What did Jesus say to us? What is his will for us to-day?' Bonhoeffer's treatment of discipleship centers around the lifestyle commended and commanded by Jesus in the Sermon on the Mount from Matthew's Gospel. The call to discipleship and the defining life centered in the cross open his treatment. Following the Sermon on the Mount Bonhoeffer seeks to position the individual disciple within the community of faith with an emphasis on the experience of the messengers of Christ and the response they can expect from their message in a hostile culture. 'When Christ calls a man, he bids him come and die.' With these words, in *The Cost of Discipleship*, Dietrich Bonhoeffer gave powerful voice to the millions of Christians who believe personal sacrifice is an essential component of faith.

A. B. Bruce. *The Training of the Twelve* (Grand Rapids: Kregel, 1971).

This fairly academic coverage of how Jesus taught his disciples is a classic, and the basis for several other more well-known books.

Henry Cloud and John Townsend. *Making Small Groups Work* (Grand Rapids: Zondervan, 2003).

This a pointed and practical book on small group dynamics and why they are so powerful in effecting life change. The authors clarify precisely how groups help people grow, the various dynamics involved in group life, the specific role and responsibilities of a good group leader, the preferred responsibilities of group members, and how to deal with the problems and challenges certain to be encountered in every group. This is a goldmine of insights from two experienced counselors/group leaders. Anyone involved in discipling others would benefit greatly from this work.

Robert E. Coleman. *The Master Plan of Evangelism* (Grand Rapids: Baker Book House Company, 1963).

While the title of this book uses the word evangelism, it's really about how Jesus made disciples. This book explores principles essential to effective disciple making in a way found nowhere else. It is a must-read. Coleman lays out 8 stages that Jesus took his disciples through to ready them for the time when he would depart, and they would represent him on earth. This book is full of insight into the biblical text, and memorable sentences that shape the disciple-making vision.

Rowland Forman, Jeff Jones, and Bruce Miller. *The Leadership Baton: An Intentional Strategy For Developing Leaders In Your Church* (Grand Rapids, Michigan: Zondervan, 2004).

Writing from the philosophy and perspective of the Fellowship Bible Church movement founded by Gene Getz, these three have founded the Center for Church Based Training which propagates the FBC approach to leadership development. Their excellent training material is interactive and suited for use in small groups and classes. The book has a section on personal mentoring that is brief but good.

Bill Hull. *Jesus Christ Disciplemaker* (Grand Rapids, Michigan: Baker Books, 1984, 2004).

This is a fine analysis of Jesus' work in making disciples. Anyone interested in making disciples should read this careful study that is full of insights on how Jesus formed character and understanding in his followers. Hull has written much over the years around this topic and all of his books will prove helpful, especially situated within the reproduction of the faith in a local church context.

Richard Longenecker. *Patterns of Discipleship* (Grand Rapids, Michigan: Eerdmans, 1996).

These essays by thirteen scholars examine what the New Testament says about the subject of discipleship. There is an emphasis on both the unity of the theme and the diversity with which it is treated in the New Testament. There are also suggestions as to how Christian discipleship can be expressed today. Sections include the biblical theological treatments from the Gospels, the Pauline corpus, and other New Testament books such as Hebrews, James, 1 Peter and Revelation. The themes of discipleship are handled exegetically and yet with great practicality for application in the present.

Greg Ogden. *Transforming Discipleship: Making Disciples a Few at a Time* (Downers Grove: IVP, 2003).

This is book born out of long-term implementation by one who has served as both a pastor and seminary teacher. Ogden analyzes Jesus' and Paul's approaches to making disciples. His section on practical strategy in the local church is especially helpful. He raises the importance of the relational dimension of disciple making, and clearly explains why programs alone cannot deliver the genuine transformation so needed. Ogden advances a method based on small groups where three people meet together. Ogden talks of the need for slow and steady growth.

As one of the most practical writers on the biblical understanding and practice of discipleship, Ogden provides a crisp, clear definition of the term, identifies the root causes of the current 'discipleship malaise' in the Evangelical Church, reviews the discipling methodologies of Jesus and Paul, and offers detailed instructions for how to disciple people to maturity. One summary statement punctuates the importance of passing the discipleship baton: 'The tragedy is that most Christian leaders have placed almost no priority on transitional leadership. It is generally fair to say that the effectiveness of one's ministry is to be measured by how well it flourishes after one's departure.' (p. 96)

J. Dwight Pentecost. *Design for Discipleship* (Grand Rapids: Kregel Publications, 1996).

The opening three chapters alone on making disciples, the call to discipleship, and becoming a disciple make this book worth the purchase price. Distinguishing the levels of dedication from the curious to the convinced to the committed, Pentecost shows from the lives of Jesus' early disciples how Christ wanted to bring them along in their faith and faithfulness. From following at a distance to full fruit-bearing, a disciple is a follower of Christ when he obeys the Word of the Lord all along the way. Related chapters treat the issues of authority, sacrifice, prayer, service, ministry, fellowship, and the relationship of a disciple to the wider world that is often hostile to Christ and his message.

J. Oswald Sanders. *Spiritual Discipleship* (Chicago: Moody Press, 1990).

Originally published under the title, *Shoe-Leather Commitment*, this book is an extended description of what it means to be a true disciple of Jesus. It focuses on committing your own life to discipleship rather than on how to make disciples of others. It is good for inspiration, and for getting a vision of committed Christian living.

Paul D. Stanley and J. Robert Clinton. *Connecting: The Mentoring Relationships You Need to Succeed in Life* (Colorado Springs: Navpress, 1992).

This is a classic discussion of mentoring in a variety of different relationships. Stanley and Clinton distinguish 'occasional mentoring' such as by teachers, counselors, from 'passive mentoring' such as role models. In this treatment, mentoring is not a synonym for personal discipleship. Their definitions are broad, and they include secular mentors in business or professions. An important point is that Christian leaders usually name more than one person as having key influence in their lives, often in different roles. The discipler, the coach, and the spiritual guide are the three most intentional types of mentors. This book ends with a stirring study on finishing well. The authors reveal disturbing findings that most leaders fail to do so.

Michael Wilkins. *Following the Master: A Biblical Theology of Discipleship* (Grand Rapids: Zondervan, 1992).

This is a fairly academic analysis of discipleship, both from the standpoint of being a disciple of Christ and raising up disciples. Wilkins has been a practitioner, and is also a professor. Wilkins traces the theme through the classical, Hellenistic, the Old Testament, and Inter-testmental periods of history as a background for his particular treatment of discipleship from the book of Matthew. His study focuses on the term 'disciple' in Matthew and then takes Peter as a sample to treat the theological meaning of discipleship from a narrative characterization perspective. This was his doctoral dissertation, so is biblically thorough and informative, as one might expect.

PART 2 • SECTION IIC-5
Diaspora (Scattered Peoples)

International Organization for Migration (IOM) World Migration Report 2011 (International Organization for Migration, 2011).

> IOM's annual *World Migration Report* is essential for studying current trends in world migration. It provides up-to-date analysis of regional migration issues, policies, and global demographic trends. The current theme is: Communicating Effectively about Migration. It is an invaluable tool for missions students, missiologists, and filed workers who are reaching out to migrants.

Doug Saunders. *Arrival City: The Final Migration and Our Next World* (Vintage Canada Edition, 2011).

> One significant result of Diaspora is massive urbanization and the growth of the city. *Arrival City*, written by one of Canada's leading journalists addresses the diversity of a people who are coming upon the 'city'. He takes readers on a tour of today's great cities, and discusses the change that migrants are bringing to the community.

Ian Goldin, Geoffrey Cameron, and Meera Balarajan. *Exceptional People: How Migration Shaped Our World and Will Define Our Future* (Princeton: Princeton University Press, 2011).

> *Exceptional People* looks at the history of migration, and its impact on societies and countries. It will give missions enthusiasts a vivid overview of migration and where it has brought us today.

Stephen Castles and Mark J. Miller. *The Age of Migration: International Population Movements in the Modern World.* 4th ed (New York: The Guilford Press, 2009).

Stéphane Dufoix. *Diasporas.* Trans. W. Rodarmor (Berkeley, California: University of California Press, 2008).

> Significant migration and the founding of diaspora communities are transforming the global landscape. These two first-rate resources by internationally-recognized experts orient the reader to basic definitions, the history of sociological and anthropological research, regional trends, and the diverse realities faced and created by these populations. Those interested in the multi-disciplinary field of diaspora missiology will inform their own research and efforts by such works.

> There are a growing number of research centers that are dedicated to diaspora and migration studies, which offer helpful and up-to-date information and case studies on diaspora theory, diaspora communities, and migration realities. Several academic journals focus on these topics, including *Diaspora: A Journal of Transnational Studies, Journal of Ethnic and Migration Studies,* and *International Migration Review.* Some journals concentrate on certain regions or populations, such as *Asian and Pacific Migration Journal* and *Notes and Records: An International Journal of African and African Diaspora Studies.*

> There are multiple internet sites tracking migration and diaspora movement and communities. Many are group or geographically specific; others offer a more general view. Note, for example, http://www.migrationinformation.org/GlobalData/ and the United Nations website on International Migration http://www.un.org/esa/population/migration

Jehu J. Hanciles. *Beyond Christendom: Globalization, African Migration, and the Transformation of the West* (Maryknoll, New York: Orbis, 2008).

> Hanciles argues that the demise of the Christendom model worldwide, economic globalization, the changes in the profile of global Christianity, and the South-North migration of millions together have triggered an unprecedented missionary reality. Newly arrived Christian communities from the African continent visualize themselves in America as the vanguard of a fresh missionary movement of God in the world. This volume combines excellent historical research and missiological analysis with impressive case studies.

Philip Jenkins. *The Next Christendom: The Coming of Global Christianity.* 3rd edition (New York: Oxford University Press, 2011).

> An important work about the shift of the center of the Christian faith to the Global South, now in its third edition. Jenkins raises awareness of the changing face of the Christian church, with theological emphases and religious practices different from what usually is seen in the West. This book can serve as a primer for those who want to get an initial feel of the kind of Christianity that is impacting the church in unexpected ways worldwide.

S. Hun Kim and Wonsuk Ma (eds). *Korean Diaspora and Christian Mission.* Regnum Studies in Mission. (Eugene, Oregon: Wipf & Stock, 2011).

Korean Diaspora and Christian Mission provides an overview of the Korean Diaspora's role in global missions. It contains Korean Diaspora case studies that will inspire other diaspora groups to strategize and mobilize for diaspora missions. This is a multi-author work on Korean diaspora movements and their missional implications. Its 21 articles cover historical, biblical, theological, and missiological explanations regarding global diasporas in general and Korean diaspora in particular. It is divided into three sections: Korean diaspora mission's (1) theological foundations (2) related subjects such as Korean Evangelicals and Muslim neighbors, and multi-ethnic ministries, and (3) case studies. A significant and useful resource for understanding and evaluating diaspora mission studies, especially in Korean diasporic contexts.

Luis Pantoja, Enoch Wan, and Sadiri Tira (eds). *Scattered: The Global Filipino Presence* (Manila, Philippines: LifeChange, 2004).

Scattered, defined 'Diaspora Missiology' as 'a missiological study of the phenomena of diaspora groups being scattered geographically and the strategy of gathering for the Kingdom'. It was the first volume to address the Filipino Diaspora and its role in global missions. *Scattered* explores the historical, biblical, theological, and practical aspects of Filipino Diaspora in global missions. A classic text on Diaspora Missiology and a must read for diaspora missions students.

Enoch Wan (ed). *Diaspora Missiology: Theory, Methodology, and Practice* (Seattle, Washington: CreateSpace, 2012).

This four-part collection of essays is an introductory volume on the theory, methodology, and practice of diaspora missiology and its sub-fields. It describes the new global demographic realities that have given rise to this new multi-discipline paradigm in missiology, which is different in significant ways from traditional missiology. In addition to a biblical and theological orientation, eight case studies demonstrate the need for and the challenge of diaspora missions as a new mission strategy. Contains extensive bibliography.

Lausanne resources: The Lausanne Movement has hosted a series of consultations on diaspora
http://www.lausanne.org/en/gatherings/issue-based/diasporas-2009.html
and has produced *Scattered to Gather: Embracing the Global Trend of Diaspora* (Manila: LifeChange Publishing Inc., 2010), which is available for download on the internet. Also note Lausanne Occasional Paper #55, *Diasporas and International Students: The New People Next Door*
http://www.lausanne.org/en/documents/lops/871-lop-55.html

Published in 2004, LOP #55 continues to provide missions students with a context for Lausanne's Diaspora initiative. The Scattered to Gather booklet contains a strategy for reaching the 'people on the move'. It was presented to the participants of Cape Town 2010. It includes a theology of Diaspora Missiology, and practical suggestions for participation at a local level. Assembled by the Lausanne Diasporas Leadership Team.

The Vatican's Pontifical Council for the Pastoral Care of Migrants and Itinerant People has resources at
http://www.vatican.va/roman_curia/pontifical_councils/migrants/index.htm

Because this is a burgeoning field in missiological circles, articles on migration, diaspora communities, and diaspora missiology appear in scholarly missiological journals, such as *Global Missiology, Transformation, Mission Studies, Missiology, International Review of Mission,* journals dedicated to geographical regions, as well as more popular level publications like *Evangelical Missions Quarterly*.

Torch Trinity Journal, Volume 13.1 & 13.2 (Seoul, Korea: TTGST, 2010).

In 2010, Torch Trinity Graduate School of Theology, Seoul, dedicated two of their journal volumes to the issue of Diaspora. These papers are vital to developing a framework for diaspora missions.

Film: Daniel Groody. *Dying to Live: A Migrant's Journey* (Groody River Films).

Dying to Live highlights the journey of Mexican migrant workers who take great risks 'to live.' In this film, Catholic priest, Daniel Groody explores the search for God amid the struggle.

PART 2 • SECTION IIC-5A
Scattered Peoples: International Students

While the majority of Diaspora peoples become permanent residents as immigrants and refugees in their new, adopted homelands, there are other internationals who are temporary residents, most of whom will eventually return home. Among them are about three million International Students and Scholars. These form a strategic sub-set of the broad category of 'scattered' or Diaspora peoples, because they represent the future leadership and nation-builders of the world.

The growth of the International Student Ministry (ISM) 'movement' has gradually accelerated in the last 60 years. It traces its roots back to 1911, when John R Mott, the leader of the 1910 World Missionary Conference, established the first national ministry among foreign students, *The Committee on Friendly Relations among Foreign Students*.

Lausanne Occasional Paper #55: *Diasporas and International Students: The New People Next Door*, 2004. Available at http://www.lausanne.org/en/documents/lops/871-lop-55.html

The LOP #55 is a joint publication of two Issue Groups (Diaspora and International Students) which met separately and collaboratively at the Lausanne 2004 Forum. The section on International Students was crafted by 23 International Student Ministry participants from 10 countries.

Leiton Edward Chinn. *International Student Ministry: From 'Blind-Spot' to Vision* (advance paper for the Lausanne Diaspora Strategy Consultation, Manila, 2009; available from the author, lechinn@aol.com).

This 21-page paper is the most comprehensive overview of the ISM movement, including the biblical-missiological perspectives and strategic nature of ISM, and the growth of the ISM movement globally (incorporating data from 57 major ISMs from 22 countries). Also included is the growth of the ISM movement within the Lausanne context, and some priorities for the future.

A modified and expanded version of the paper was incorporated into *Making Disciples of International Students in Global Migration*, a paper for the Tokyo2010: Global Mission Consultation.

Lawson Lau. *The World at Your Doorstep: A Handbook for International Student Ministry* (Downers Grove, Illinois: IVP, 1984), and *God Brings the World to Your Doorstep: Open Your Heart and Home to Welcome the Internationals* (self-published by Dr. Lawson Lau, 2006; lawsonllau@gmail.com).

Peter Morrison. *A Christian's Pocket Guide to the Chinese* (Christian Focus Publications / OMF International, 2008).

John Taylor and Hugh Trevor. *A Christian's Pocket Guide to the Japanese* (Christian Focus Publications / OMF International, 2008).

Dr. Lawson Lau, a journalist and international graduate student from Singapore to the United States in the 1980s, shares his personal experience and lessons and practical advice for ISM in his first volume, and adds additional insights 22 years later in his second work. Both books are used by the author for a seminary course on ISM.

The Christian's Guide titles, both short books, are written by westerners with years of immersion in the host culture, and years of ministry among students. Each covers political, cultural and religious backgrounds, and in short chapters engages with the questions and the aspects of culture shock a Chinese / Japanese student would encounter in the West. Pithy, practical and highly commended.

Tom Phillips and Bob Norsworthy. *The World at Your Door: Reaching International Students in Your Home, Church, and School* (Minneapolis, Minnesota: Bethany House Publishers, 1997).

Nearly 45 years of collective organizational experiences and resources of International Students Inc are gleaned by the former ISI leaders in compiling this tool chest for churches, ministries, and individuals interested or engaged in ISM.

Catherine Weston. *Mission Possible: Reaching the World on Our Doorstep; The Story of Friends International* (self-published, 2006. Available from catherine@intonations.org).

This is an historical account of the establishing of the UK's oldest and largest national ISM with a focus for equipping churches for outreach among international students.

Special Concern of ISMs: A survey of regional ISMs (North America, Asia-Pacific; and Greater Europe) disclosed the priority issue of 'Reentry' to countries of origin and the challenges faced by 'Returnees'. Some International Student Reentry resources have been developed for preparing Christian international students for growth and service as returnees.

Lisa Espineli Chinn. *Think Home: A Re-entry Guide for Christian International Students* (Madison, Wisconsin: International Student Ministry, InterVarsity/USA, 2011; first edition 1984, revised 1987, 2000).

Think Home was the first reentry/returnee publication for Christian international students, and it has been adapted by ISMs in more than five countries and modified for use by other ISMs in North America. A companion volume by the author, *Back Home: Daily Reflections on Reentry for Those Who Lived and Studied Abroad* (2011) is also available at http://www.intervarsity.org/ism, as well as Chinn's *Customs and Culture*, the only reentry simulation, role-play game.

Nate Mirza. *Home Again: Preparing International Students to Serve Christ in Their Home Countries* (Colorado Springs, CO: Dawson Media, 2005, first edition 1993).

The experiences and advice of returnees to South-East Asia culled from numerous interviews in their homelands contribute significantly to this practical handbook for spiritual growth and ministry.

Leiton Edward Chinn. *International Student Reentry & Returnee Ministry: An Overview* (article written for ChinaSource Journal, 2011). Available at lechinn@aol.com

The research and resources section of the paper lists several Christian publications pertaining to international and nation-specific (e.g. China) returning students.

Websites for ISM Organizations and Resources:

Association of Christians Ministering among Internationals (North America): http://www.acmi-net.net

International Students Inc (USA): http://www.isionline.org

Friends International (UK): http://www.friendsinternational.org.uk

ISM New Zealand: http://www.ism.org.nz/

International Student Ministries Canada: http://www.ismc.ca

International Student Ministry/Intervarsity USA: http://www.intervarsity.org/ism

For websites of 57 major ISMs in 22 countries, see above: Leiton Edward Chinn. *International Student Ministry: From 'Blind-Spot' to Vision*

For the most comprehensive lists of ISM related resources and websites, contact Ned Hale: nhale@intervarsity.org.

PART 2 • SECTION IIC-6
Religious Freedom

Peter Kuzmic. 'To Suffer with Our Lord: Christian Responses to Religious Persecution,' *The Review of Faith & International Affairs*, 2(3), 2004-2005, 35-42.

> Writing primarily for an American audience, Croatian theologian and social commentator Peter Kuzmic addresses the lack of serious theological reflection on the issue of persecution. He argues 'American Christians hear much more about prosperity than persecution, success than suffering, wealth and health than poverty and pain. Influenced by the general culture of optimism, many Christians—evangelicals and charismatics in particular—have developed a theology of success at the expense of a theology of the Cross.' Drawing on Lausanne Covenant article 13 and his own experience of ethno-religious conflict in the Balkans, Kuzmic sketches a Christian view of suffering caused by religious persecution.

Ronald Boyd-MacMillan. *Faith That Endures: The Essential Guide to the Persecuted Church* (Grand Rapids: Revell, 2006).

H. Knox Thames. *International Religious Freedom Advocacy: A Guide to Organizations, Law, and NGOs* (Waco: Baylor University Press, 2009).

> These two books are ideal for those interested in thoughtfully aiding the persecuted Evangelical Christians wrote both books, though Thames writes for a general audience. A leading religious freedom legal expert, Thames shows would-be advocates 'the path from their home to the international stage.' After examining the corpus of international law on religious freedom and the variety of ways governments violates those laws, the author surveys the multilateral organizations and U.S. government entities relevant to religious freedom advocacy.

> For readers eager to more deeply understand and more effectively assist the persecuted church, Boyd-MacMillan's *Faith That Endures* is the best resource of its kind. He takes readers on an educational, engaging, and evocative journey into the lives of beleaguered believers around the world—setting real-life personal stories of persecution and perseverance within an analytical framework of four ideological engines of persecution: religious nationalism, transnational Islamic extremism, totalitarian insecurity, and secular intolerance.

Restrictions on Religion (Pew Forum on Religion and Public Life)

Annual Report on International Religious Freedom (U.S. State Department)

> Many organizations, including Christian religious freedom groups, publish annual reports on persecution. Some feature a few select countries or focus on a particular religious group. Quality varies greatly. For an excellent graphical summary of the state of religious freedom, turn to the *Restrictions on Religion* report published by the Pew Forum on Religion and Public Life. The report looks at both social hostilities and government restrictions in global, regional, and national context. The best narrative summary of global religious freedom is produced by the U.S. State Department. Their *Annual Report on International Religious Freedom* is the only comprehensive report that covers all religions in all countries every year. Each country report provides information on religious demographics, law and policy, ongoing restrictions on and specific abuses of religious freedom, and actions the U.S. government has taken to advance religious freedom in that country. The Report's dry bureaucratic language does not make for scintillating reading and preserves and objective, factual style.

Review of Faith and International Affairs (Global Engagement)

International Journal of Religious Freedom (International Institute for Religious Freedom)

Bad Urach Call (International Institute for Religious Freedom)

Fides et Libertas (International Religious Liberty Association)

> Most religious freedom organizations publish a magazine or newsletter featuring their work around the world. Too many of these publications tend to sensationalize their reporting, thus giving readers a distorted view of religious persecution around the world. Three journals stand out as the most credible publications.

The *Review of Faith & International Affairs* is a quarterly, peer-reviewed journal published by the Washington-based Institute for Global Engagement, an evangelical organization. While RFIA does not focus singularly on religious freedom, articles related to that topic can be found in nearly every issue. The journal is aimed at both scholars and practitioners, and contributors represent a wide variety of religious traditions. The full text is only available by subscription, though select articles are available for free online.

The *International Journal of Religious Freedom* (IJRF) is an excellent, scholarly Christian journal published twice a year by the International Institute for Religious Freedom (IIRF). IJRF gives voice to non-Western Christian perspectives and highlights the theological and missiological dimensions of religious persecution. All IJRF issues are available online. Students can also avail themselves of the IIRF's *Bad Urach Call* on suffering, persecution, and martyrdom, as well as the many other resources on its website.

Fides et Libertas is a scholarly journal published annually by the International Religious Liberty Association, which has close links to the Seventh-day Adventists. All previous issues going back to 2000 are available for free online.

THE CAPE TOWN CALL TO ACTION

UNIT 10

PART 2 • SECTION IID-1
Unreached Peoples

Alan Johnson. 'Analyzing the Frontier Mission Movement and Unreached People Group Thinking. Part I: The Frontier Mission Movement's Understanding of the Modern Mission Era.' *International Journal of Frontier Missions* 18 no 2 (Summer 2001), 81–8. Part II can be found in the same issue pp. 89-97.

Joshua Project. http://www.joshuaproject.net

Nik Repkin. 'Why Are the Unreached Unreached?' *Evangelical Missions Quarterly* 32 no 3 (1996), 284–8.

Harley Schreck and David Barrett (eds). *Unreached Peoples' Clarifying the Task* (Monrovia, MARC, 1987).

Ralph Winter. 'Finishing the Task: The Unreached Peoples Challenge.' in *Perspectives on the World Christian Movement: A Reader*, 531-46. (Pasadena: William Carey Library, 2009). This article can also be access via the *International Journal of Frontier Missions* 16 (April-June 1999), 67–76 or online at http://www.internationalbulletin.org

The resources listed in this section are helpful in gaining more information regarding unreached people groups and how to reach them effectively. Schreck and Barrett present the foundational concerns history and resources in Part I of their book and dedicate Part II to unreached people in Africa. Winter's article traces the progress of the Gospel through history. It highlights the scriptural mandate for reaching all people groups, and provides clarifying information on the definition of people groups. It treats the presence and location of people groups in the world, as well as guiding the reader into strategic thinking on how to reach them. The Joshua Project website provides information on people groups globally. Information may also be found on The Lausanne Movement's website: http://www.lausanne.org.

For those who wish to find translations of sacred literature from other religions, the following will be helpful. The texts below, mostly in English, offer good starting points for study.

For Hinduism:

Annie Besant, trans. *The Bhagavad Gita: Text and Translation.* 1904. 17th Reprint (Chennai: The Theosophical Publishing House, 1998).

Wendy Doniger. *Hindu Myths* (London: Penguin Books, 1975).

R. C. Dutt, trans. *Ramayana* (New Delhi: Rupa Co., n.d.).

Ralph T. H. Griffith, trans. *The Hymns of the Ṛgveda* Ed J.L. Shastri, 1973. Reprint (Deli: Banarsidass Publishers, 2004).

Raimundo Panikkar. *The Vedic Experience, Mantramanjari: An Anthology of the Vedas for Modern Man and Contemporary Celebration* (Berkeley and Los Angeles: University of California Press, 1977).

S. Radhakrishnan, trans. *The Principle Upanishad* (Great Britain: George Allen & Unwin Ltd., 1953; Reprint, New Delhi: Harper Collins, 1999).

For Buddhism:

Donald S. Lopez Jr. (ed). *Buddhist Scriptures* (London: Penguin Books, 2004).

For Islam:

A. J. Arberry, trans. *The Koran Interpreted* (New York: Simon & Schuster, 1996).

Majid Fakhry, trans. *An Interpretation of the Qur'an: English Translations of the Meanings a Bilingual Edition* (New York: New York University Press, 2004).

For Taoism (Daoism):

Martin Palmer, trans. *The Book of Chuang Tzu* (London: Penguin Books, 2006).

D. C. Lau, trans. *Lau Tzu: Tau Te Ching* (London: Penguin Books, 1963).

PART 2 • SECTION IID-2
Orality

The initial two entries cover general issues in cross-cultural communication that serve as a context for orality.

David Hesselgrave. *Communicating Christ Cross-Culturally* (Grand Rapids, Michigan: Zondervan, 1978).

As missionary and scholar, Hesselgrave examines literature on communication science to assist those carrying the gospel across cultures. He explains the role of culture in communication, contextualization. This work is widely used as a resource in the church, on campus, and among mission organizations.

Paul G. Hiebert. *Anthropological Insights for Missionaries* (Grand Rapids, Michigan: Baker Book House, 1985); *The Gospel in Human Contexts* (Grand Rapids, Michigan: Baker Book House, 2009); *Transforming Worldviews* (Grand Rapids, Michigan: Baker Book House, 2008).

In these three works, mission practitioner and professor appeals for the necessity of exegesis—both Scripture exegesis and human exegesis, the process of understanding the gospel and the people to whom we take it. Given the world of oral cultures, these books look at the ways one would understand human context and communicate faithfully the gospel to the unreached.

ION/The Lausanne Movement. *Making Disciples of Oral Learners* (Pattya, Thailand: The Lausanne Movement, 2005).

This is the formative work of the modern orality movement. Mission leaders collaborate to introduce the challenge and solution of communicating the gospel to oral cultures. This work explains the who, what, where, and why of the need for the orality movement.

Orality Breakouts (Hong Kong: ION/The Lausanne Movement, 2010).

After the dawn of the orality movement, these global case studies were compiled from the frontier of the unreached to demonstrate the 'how' of using oral-based strategies to reach the billions who learn Scripture and gospel content through oral methods.

Herbert V. Klem. *Oral Communication of the Scripture* (Pasadena, CA: William Carey Library, 1982).

Using insight from African oral art, the author argues oral communication strategies must be employed for the gospel to be heard and understood by the world of oral cultures.

Paul F. Koehler. *Telling God's Story with Power: Biblical Storytelling in Oral Cultures* (Pasadena: William Carey Library, 2010).

Koehler introduces orality, explains biblical storytelling, and describes findings from case studies and research conducted among oral communities. This book is filled with numerous accounts of tribal, rural, and other oral cultures that prefer to learn through orality. This is a practical introduction to storying, focused on those who desire to learn how to use storytelling in cross-cultural contexts and train others to become biblical storytellers. It includes many fascinating accounts of the responses of tribal people to the gospel via storying. It is based on years of research and field testing of various aspects of storying.

Lesslie Newbigin. *Foolishness to the Greeks* (Grand Rapids, Michigan: Eerdmans, 1986).

A classic by a missionary statesman, this landmark work challenges the reader to examine the issues raised in cross-cultural communication of the gospel. He challenges the reader to understand how a culture's great pillars (science, politics, and other sectors) should be confronted with the claims of the gospel.

Walter J. Ong. *Orality and Literacy: The Technologizing of the World* (Methuen & Co. Ltd., 182. Reprint, London: Routledge: 2006).

Landmark work distinguishing orality and literacy and the cultures that embody the characteristics of each. Ong explores the profound difference between oral and literate cultures. Ong argues that oral communication transforms thought patterns, speech patterns, memory, and cultural consciousness. He offers an account of the intellectual, literary and social effects of writing, print and electronic technology. Ong offers insights into oral genres across the globe; he examines the rise of abstract philosophical and scientific thinking, and the impact of orality-literacy studies on literary criticism and theory. He also considers our understanding of what it is to be a human being, conscious of self and other.

Avery Willis and Mark Snowden. *Truth that Sticks* (Colorado Springs: Navpress, 2010).

From the unreached billions among oral cultures around the world, these authors bring oral communication strategy home to discuss and propose a working model of reaching and discipling through the orality preferences we all share. Willis and Snowden build a model for discipleship and evangelism through orality based small groups.

Harriet Hill. 'Conversations About Orality', *Missiology: An International Review* 38 (2010): pp. 215-217.

Experienced translator and consultant, Hill takes a question and answer approach to orality issues, talking about the recent history, ministries involved in orality as well as missiological issues. She includes a section on what could strengthen the orality movement.

International Journal of Frontier Missions special issue on Reaching Non-Literate Peoples (Volume 12:3, 1995). Available for download at http://www.ijfm.org
Articles include:

Dependence on Literacy Strategy, Herb V. Klem

The Crucial Role of Oral-Scripture, Gilbert Ansre

The Emergence of Audio-Scripture in Church and Mission, Viggo Sogaard

Audio-Communications and the Progress of the Gospel, Allan Starling

Was Jesus a Zairian?, Paul D. Dyer

The Role of the O.T. in Evangelism, Don Pederson

Storying the Storybook to Tribals, Tom A. Steffen

Philip A. Noss. 'The Oral Story and Bible Translation,' *The Bible Translator* 27 (1981): 301-318.

Rick Brown. 'Communicating God's Message in an Oral Culture,' *International Journal of Frontier Missions*, 21:3, 122-128.

Based on his extensive experiences in Africa and Asia, and in Bible translation and consulting, Brown examines core principles for communicating biblical truth in primarily oral cultures. He describes the way oral and print cultures learn and communicate, and the implications on the communication of biblical truth, as well as how the Bible readily lends itself to primarily oral cultures.

Tom A. Steffen. 'A Narrative Approach to Communicating the Bible, Part 1,' *Christian Education Journal* 24 (1994): pp. 86-97.

Tom A. Steffen. 'A Narrative Approach to Communicating the Bible, Part 2,' *Christian Education Journal* 24 (1994): pp. 98-109.

Tom A. Steffen. 'Paradigm Changes for Effective Evangelism,' *Evangelism: A Lausanne Cooperating Periodical* 9 (1994): pp. 136-140.

Tom A. Steffen and Tom and J.O. Terry. 'The Sweeping Story of Scripture Taught Through Time,' *Missiology: An International Review* 35 (2007): pp. 315-335.

Steffen and Terry give a carefully-researched run both through the current orality history (with excellent bibliographic information) and how leaders throughout history used oral methods.

Jacob A. Loewen. *Culture and Human Values* (Pasadena: William Carey Library, 1975).

Loewen's experience on the ground in Africa as a language and culture expert bring amazing, if not controversial, perspectives. His chapter 'Bible Stories: Message and Matrix' is a very good chapter on interaction with oral peoples.

Leighton Ford. *The Power of Story. Rediscovering the Oldest, Most Natural Way to Reach People for Christ* (Colorado Springs: NavPress, 1994).

In this age of high-tech communication and endless formulas for successful evangelism, the most effective way to lead others to Christ is, surprisingly, also the oldest, purest, and most natural; the same way that Jesus, Paul, and all the early evangelists told of the great work of God. Ford explains how you can experience the joy of leading others to Christ: simply by telling them the story of how God has impacted your life. Ford weaves a tale of three friends through the book whose lives are touched, one by one, by the power of God's Story.

Paul H. DeNeui (ed). *Communicating Christ Through Story and Song: Orality in Buddhist Contexts* (Pasadena: William Carey Library, 2008).

Communicating Christ Through Story and Song, the fifth and latest volume in the Buddhist World series, presents models and case studies of communication of the Gospel through orality in Southeast Asia. With contributions from seasoned practitioners working in Cambodia, Thailand, Sri Lanka, Bhutan, and the Philippines, this insightful book explores the biblical foundations – and the cultural imperative – of employing oral tradition to effectively communicate in Buddhist contexts.

Tom A. Steffen. *Reconnecting God's Story to Ministry: Crosscultural Storytelling at Home and Abroad* (Waynesboro, GA: Authentic Media, 2005).

Steffen helps readers see the value of storytelling for evangelism-discipleship. The book provides practical help by identifying the roles and tasks necessary to become an effective storyteller in another culture. Steffen offers creative tools and introduces practical ways to increase many of the storytelling skills. He moves beyond a linear gospel, Western logic, Western organization, and individual responses to traditional evangelism rituals. He speaks of a mode of communication that respects the audience, making it easy for them to grasp what they have heard and to pass it on to others with minimal loss of content.

Viggo Søgaard. *Media in Church and Mission: Communicating the Gospel* (Pasadena: William Carey Library, 1993).

While written before much of the revolution in digital media, this book provides useful strategic input for those involved in media and Scripture Engagement.

Vincent J. Donovan. *Christianity Rediscovered* (Maryknoll, New York: Orbis, 1978).

Donovan was a Catholic missioner working among the Maasai people in Kenya. He tried to teach them the usual church traditions then discovered that they were oral people who quickly caught on to Bible stories. It is very interesting to watch Donovan's progression of understanding and faith. Beyond the orality issues, this profound and thought-provoking book is one of the classics of modern missionary writing. That is in part for what is outlines with relation to the method and content of evangelism; the meaning of the eucharist; and the nature of ministry. We are led back to consider the question of our understanding of the mission of the church in all its contexts.

Daniel R. Sanchez, J.O. Terry and Lanette W. Thompson. *Bible Storying for Church Planting* (Fort Worth, Texas: Church Starting Network, 2008).

Bible Storying is being used increasingly for evangelism and Christian nurture. This book takes a forward step in showing how it can be used in the exciting opportunity of starting new congregations. J.O. Terry also has a series of works in this regard, in the Church Starting Network (CSN):

1999   *Grief Stories from the Bible* (Fort Worth, Texas: CSN)
2000   *Water Stories from the Bible* (Fort Worth, Texas: CSN)
2003   *Death Stories from the Bible* (Fort Worth, Texas: CSN)

2008   *Basic Bible Storying* (Fort Worth, Texas: CSN)
2008   *Bible Storying Handbook for Short-Term Mission Teams and Mission Volunteers* (Fort Worth, Texas: CSN)
2009   *Food Stories from the Bible* (Fort Worth, Texas: CSN)
2009   *Hope Stories from the Bible* (Fort Worth, Texas: CSN)

Note: (http://www.churchstarting.net/biblestorying/Books.htm) includes many specific examples of Bible stories and outlines. These tools will help you develop stories from the Bible.

Walk Thru the Bible. *Story Thru the Bible: An Interactive Way to Connect with God's Word* (Colorado Springs, Colorado: NavPress, 2011).

This approach to storying began in the 1980s. It uses word pictures and images for telling the whole story of the Bible. The WTB materials are translated into many languages. Their seminars have trained many people in the OT and / or NT. These studies have been offered by local people around the world. You can see where they work at http://www.walkthru.org/where-we-work

Scriptures in Use. *The Ancient Path: Church Planting Training for Oral Cultures* (Scriptures in Use, 2004).

A Scripture-based, narrative approach for grassroots church planters on DVD. It provides a brief overview of how members of traditional oral cultures learn and communicate information. This resource introduces strategies that complement traditional communication methods such as storytelling, drama, music, recitation, and oratory. You will observe scripture storytellers and church planting teams in action and walk briefly through 10 bridges of communication to oral cultures that are taught in the BRIDGES training workshops. The Scriptures in Use training is done globally, seeking to train local trainers in oral Scripture communications methods.

Other key websites and downloadable resources include:

Chronological Story Telling for Kids, http://www.cbs4kids.org

John Walsh, accomplished Bible story teller, http://www.christianstorytelling.com

http://www.churchstarting.net/biblestorying/Books.htm

Youth and Storying, http://www.echothestory.com

Following Jesus: Making Disciples of Oral Learners, http://www.fjseries.org/low/home.html

Making Disciples of Oral Learners, http://www.lausanne.org/documents/2004forum/LOP54_IG25.pdf (downloadable book)

One Story, http://www.onestory.org

International Orality Network, http://www.oralbible.com/

Chronological Bible Teaching, http://www.ntmbooks.com/chronological_teaching

Simply the Story, http://www.simplythestory.org

Scriptures in Use, http://www.siutraining.org

Story for All podcast, http://story4all.com

Walk Thru the Bible, http://www.walkthru.org

See also: *International Journal of Frontier Missions* special issue on Reaching Non-Literate Peoples (Volume 12:3, 1995). It is available for download at http://www.ijfm.org

Part 2 • Section IID-3
Christ-centered Leadership

David W. Bennett. *Metaphors of Ministry: Biblical Images for Leaders and Followers* (Eugene, Oregon: Wipf & Stock, 2004).

Bennett examines New Testament images and metaphors relating to the way disciples follow Jesus, and in turn influence others. Based on his considerable cross-cultural experience, Bennett's aim is to stimulate deeper thinking on Christ-centered leadership for the global Church in our own day.

James M. Kouzes and Barry Z. Posner. *The Leadership Challenge* (Hoboken, New Jersey: Jossey-Bass, 2002).

This book represents the best research currently available on the most critical competencies for effective leadership of any background in any sphere. Based on observing thousands of leaders worldwide, the authors have identified five critical competencies: (i) inspiring a shared vision, (ii) challenging the process, (iii) enabling others to act, (iv) modeling the way, and (v) encouraging the heart. In their subsequent *Christian Reflections on The Leadership Challenge* the authors discuss the biblical basis for their competencies.

Edgar H. Schein. *Organizational Culture and Leadership* (Hoboken, New Jersey: Jossey Bass, 2004).

Richard W. Sessoms and Colin D. Buckland. *Culture Craft: Leading for Organizational Health.* Prepared for Lausanne Younger Leaders' Gathering, 2006. Available for download at http://christian-leadership.org/shop/#culture-craft

These books address a most critical aspect of leadership in the 21st century: the creation and care of organizational culture. Schein's extensive research is the recognized standard in the field of leadership and organizational culture. Sessoms and Buckland apply key aspects of Schein's work to leaders who want to foster a Christ-centered (healthy) organizational culture.

Future Leadership: A Call to Develop Christ-like Leaders. Lausanne Occasional Paper from 2004 Pattaya Forum. Available for free downloaded at http://www.lausanne.org/en/documents/lops/856-lop-41.html

This paper reflects a vision that energized the Lausanne Future Leadership Issue Group in Pattaya, Thailand. Here 130 participants from 43 nations worked to create a catalytic resource for developing Christ-like leaders globally. It addresses barriers, opportunities, and resources for the task of developing future leaders.

J. Robert Clinton. *The Making of a Leader: Recognizing the Lessons and Stages of Leadership Development* (Colorado Springs: NavPress, 1988).

Based on his doctoral research in the field of leadership emergence, Clinton chronicles dynamic patterns and processes in life and ministry that form Christ-centered leaders. While Clinton's research focused on vocational Christian leaders, most of his conclusions also apply to volunteers in churches and ministry organizations.

Cynthia D. McCauley, Russ S. Moxley, and Ellen Van Velsor (eds). *The Center for Creative Leadership Handbook of Leadership Development* (Hoboken, New Jersey: Jossey-Bass, 1998).

Richard W. Sessoms. *My Journey toward Understanding Leadership Development.* Available for free download at http://www.freedomtolead.net/index.php/resources/leadership-development/my-journey-toward-understandig-leadership-development/

The Center for Creative Leadership gathered chapters from numerous specialists to provide a comprehensive panorama of leadership development processes and programs used in organizations. The authors offer some evaluation of the effectiveness of these. Sessoms' narrative captures both his personal journey to understand leadership development, and a summary of his doctoral research which includes rare data on the real effectiveness – and ineffectiveness – of various types of leadership development.

Part 2 • Section IID-3A
Evangelism & Christian Leadership

The church's ministry can be greatly enhanced or seriously curtailed by the strength or weakness of its leadership. It takes good leaders to envision and empower people for evangelism, through which the gospel of Jesus Christ can be shared in humility and hope. While the number of books on the subject is vast, not all display biblical rootedness or spiritual maturity. We commend the following:

Ajith Fernando. *Jesus Driven Ministry* (Leicester: IVP, 2002).

This uplifting book is about the heart and character of the Christian leader. Fernando argues that the greatest crisis facing the church is that of lifestyle, not of technique. Questionable lifestyle is an affront to the gospel and it impedes its spread, whereas noble character is a powerful magnet for the gospel. Fernando begins by stressing the importance of the virtue of compassion in ministry, the value of experiencing the power of the Spirit, the necessity of affirming God's call into ministry. He then explores essential pastoral principles in detail, such as: discipling, mentoring, Sabbathing, 'gospel'ing, praying, crucifying the flesh, devoting oneself to Scripture, visiting in homes and hospitals, waging spiritual warfare. It cuts to the heart of the subject, which is the heart of the leader.

Ajith Fernando. *An Authentic Servant* (*Didasko Files* series. Peabody, Massachusetts: Lausanne Library / Hendrickson, 2012). This is a contracted version of the above, with questions for reflection and discussion. A stimulating and searching read.

John Stott. *Calling Christian Leaders: Biblical Models of Church, Gospel and Ministry* (Leicester: IVP, 2002).

John Stott found that models of Christian leadership are more often shaped by the surrounding culture than by Christ. In this lucid exposition of 1 Corinthians 1-4 he urges that leadership be determined by our view of the gospel and the Church, demonstrating the centrality of the theme of 'power through weakness'. He expounds the role of the Holy Spirit in God's revelation, and examines four of Paul's most striking models of ministry, each of which is an aspect of humility. Stott urges Christian leaders to be 'Christian leaders', shaped above all else by 'the meekness and the gentleness of Christ'. This is vintage Stott, lucid, profound and edifying.

Michael Green. *Evangelism in the Early Church* (Grand Rapids, Michigan: Eerdmans, 1970).

This classic study on the early church requires some dedication but is well worth it. He explains different elements of evangelism (pathways, obstacles, evangel, conversion, evangelists, methods, motives, and strategy) and assesses the strengths and weaknesses of the evangelistic approaches used by the earliest Christians. He also considers obstacles to evangelism, using outreach to Gentiles and to Jews as examples of approaches to differing contexts. Carefully-researched and frequently quoting primary sources, this book shows what can be learned from the past, and helps renew evangelistic vision.

Robert Coleman. *The Master Plan of Evangelism* (Grand Rapids: Revel, 1993).

Coleman, in this valuable and instructive book, takes us back to Jesus' practice, and from that draws important lessons for the practice of evangelism today. He calls us to view evangelism as a lifestyle rather than a communications project. He identifies eight principles that Jesus embodied in his disciple-making: Selection, Association, Consecration, Impartation, Demonstration, Delegation, Supervision, and Reproduction—and devotes a chapter to each. This book allows Jesus the Master to teach his disciples the way evangelism is to be carried out. It will help one sink deep roots into the Jesus model of evangelism.

J. Oswald Sanders. *Spiritual Leadership: Principles of Excellence for Every Believer* (Chicago: Moody, 2007).

Leighton Ford. *Transforming Leadership: Jesus' Way of Creating Vision, Shaping Values and Empowering Change* (Downers Grove: IVP, 1991).

David Watson. *I Believe in Evangelism* (London: Hodder & Stoughton, 1976).

Ron Sider. *Evangelism and Social Action* (London: Hodder & Stoughton, 1993).

Sanders and Ford have become classics in the field of Christian leadership development. Sound leadership for the Church should be shaped by Jesus, and by lessons learned from biblical characters. Both authors assist our understanding of how those principles can and ought to be worked out in the contemporary world. Watson and Sider are clear and clarion calls to engage in evangelism. Watson gives us a sound theology for evangelism while Sider extends that to include social action as an integral part of Christ's missionary call. Put together one gets a well-rounded picture of what the church in the world is called to be and do.

PART 2 • SECTION IID-4
Cities

Raymond J. Bakke. *Street Signs: A New Direction in Urban Ministry* (Birmingham, Alabama: New Hope Publications, 2006).

This draws on consultations with urban ministry practitioners in over 200 cities worldwide, and shows how to mobilize resources for urban ministry. It offers models that work.

Ray Bakke has lived and taught urban ministry since early days when he showed it really is possible to raise a family and live in urban contexts. (See The *Urban Christian*. Downers Grove, Illinois: IVP, 1987). Bakke went on to found the Bakke Graduate University http://www.bgu.edu/index.html. Its Masters in Global Urban Leadership includes Urban Immersion Programs in several of the world's cities.

Raymond J. Bakke. *A Theology as Big as the City* (Downers Grove, Illinois: IVP, 1997).

Still a masterful theological treatment of the basis of city-focused ministry, by one who has also done the work on the ground and worked with many others to improve their own urban ministries.

Billy Graham School of Missions and Evangelism. *The Journal of Urban Ministry*.

The school publishes issues on urban evangelism in a variety of world religious contexts. June, 2011 was 'Islam and the City.' David Sills and Jeffrey Walker are professors at the school which is a part of Southern Baptist Seminary, Louisville, Kentucky. http://urbanministrytraining.org

David Claerbaut. *Urban Ministry in a New Millennium* (Waynesboro, Georgia: Authentic Ministries, 2005).

Claerbaut integrates a deep understanding of sociological and demographic issues as they relate to urban areas. He is based in Chicago, writes and leads seminars widely. Contributor to Congress on Urban Ministry. See SCUPE below.

Harvie Conn and Manuel Ortiz. *The Kingdom, The City and the People of God* (Downers Grove, Illinois: IVP, 2001).

Conn was the long time professor of missions at Westminster Theological Seminary after earlier serving in Korea. He teams up with Ortiz also a professor at WTS with extensive experience in ministry among Hispanics in Chicago and Philadelphia. This work, as the title suggests, provides a complete biblical theology of the city in the mind and program of God and the responsibility and opportunity of God's people to respond to what God is doing in the cities of the World.

DAWN. (Discipling a Whole Nation) http://www.dawnministries.org

DAWN has work in 32 European nations, the Middle East, North Africa and Asia. They began in the Philippines in the 1970s following a model similar to the very successful national evangelism programs by Evangelism in Depth that targeted whole nations in Latin America Mission beginning in the 1960s. DAWN can provide extensive research on understanding the religious situation in a particular country with a view to mobilizing all Christian resources to reach a whole nation. This usually involves major urban areas as well. Of particular use for evangelism planners is *The DAWN Research Handbook* 2001 available free for downloading from the above website.

John Fuder (ed). *A Heart for the City* (Chicago: Moody Publications, 2005).

Fuder is a professor at Moody Bible Institute, and gathers an inspiring and instructive set of case studies of effective ministries in the Chicago Metroplex.

Tim Keller. http://www.redeemercitytocity.com

Tim Keller leads the Redeemer Presbyterian Church of New York City. In addition to writing books on Christian life and responsibility in the city, Keller founded Redeemer City to City (http://redeemercitytocity.com). This movement has planted or assisted in the planting of over 200 urban churches worldwide. Their website includes timely articles and blogs on understanding God's global priorities in urban contexts.

Lausanne Occasional Papers (LOPs)

LOP #9: *Christian Witness to Large Cities*. Significant documents prepared by international leaders and practitioners in urban evangelism for the Consultation on World Evangelism at Pattaya, Thailand in 1980. These remain essential reading. The report contains 135 cases of city ministries worldwide. This commission was chaired by Dr Ray Bakke, previously noted for his extensive involvement in urban ministry leadership.

SCUPE. (Seminary Consortium for Urban Pastoral Education) http://www.scupe.org

This Chicago-based consortium, begun in 1976, consists of 10 seminaries and ten denominations devoted to understanding urban ministry and preparing workers for cities anywhere. They convene the Congress on Urban Ministry which gathers ministry input from city ministries worldwide and from across North America.

PART 2 • SECTION IID-5
Children

Video: *It's Time to Wake Up*, 4/14 Window Movement, 2011. http://4to14window.com/time-to-wake-up

This video was prepared by the 4/14 Window Global Initiative. (The 4/14 Window refers to the demographic group from age four to fourteen years, which, it is argued, is the most open and receptive group to every form of spiritual and developmental input.) The video urges a new missional focus: the 4/14 Window as a golden age of opportunity to transform the world, and challenge the way we view children and their place in God's Kingdom. In God's hands, this enormous and largely-ignored people group can become agents of transformational mission under the headship of Jesus Christ.

Video: *TODAY*, 2010. http://www.max7.org/resource.aspx?id=3460bd87-b9aa-46dd-8d1d-0a0073a50888

This was prepared for the Cape Town 2010 Lausanne/WEA Congress by the Children's Team (a partnership of the Global Children's Forum, Viva and 4/14 Window Movement) as a tool to inspire leaders, churches and ministries. It presents the big picture of children in the Bible and across the world, without shying away from the challenges children are facing.

Video: *Aim Lower*, 2005. http://www.max7.org/resource.aspx?id=8af75003-cc12-4ecc-848a-4fdd4fb82fe2

A video to help churches, leaders and organizations communicate why it is vital to focus on children. It was produced as a challenging summary of the LOP issuing from the topic of Evangelization of Children at the 2004 Forum for World Evangelization. The conference was hosted by The Lausanne Movement in Pattaya, Thailand, September 29 to October 5, 2004.

Lausanne Papers:

Lausanne Occasional Paper #47. *Evangelization of Children*, 2004.
http://www.lausanne.org/en/documents/lops/862-lop-47.html

Cape Town 2010 Advance Papers (Discussion): *There Are No Unreached Children* (The Children's Team, 2010).
http://conversation.lausanne.org/en/conversations/detail/10350

Articles:

Keith White et al (eds). *Now and Next: a theological conference on Children*, 9-12 March, 2011, Nairobi, Kenya.
http://hcd-alliance.org/resources/books/doc_details/112-now-a-next

These papers arose out of the international gathering in Nairobi, Kenya, with the aim of doing 'sustained and serious theological and missiological reflection in which children and young people are seen as agents of God's mission, and as lenses through which we find, with the help of the Holy Spirit, new insights into God in Christ.' Eight organizations were involved; the Child Theology Movement (CTM), celebrating its 10th birthday; the International Fellowship for Mission as Transformation (INFEMIT) its 35th anniversary.

The 4/14 Global Summit looked to Now and Next to deepen its theological and missiological roots. It was an outcome of the Cape Town 2010 Congress.

Roy Zuck. *Precious in His Sight*, Baker Books, Grand Rapids, Michigan, 1996. Alongside is recommended: Dan Brewster. Workbook: *Children & Childhood in the Bible* (Revised Edition, Compassion, Penang, 2011).

Zuck is excellent in examining on the biblical text for understanding childhood and children. Dan Brewster's revised and updated workbook *Children & Childhood in the Bible* is designed to accompany this book, to help readers dig deep into the Bible. This workbook may be used for private study or as an instruction tool for workshops in churches, amongst child-care workers, or in other settings.

Douglas McConnell, Jennifer Orona, and Paul Stockley (eds). *Understanding God's Heart for Children: Toward a Biblical Framework* (Colorado Springs: Authentic, 2007).

McConnell provides a strong theological and missiological basis to enable church leaders, ministry workers and practitioners to care for and nurture children, and to allow them to develop, and to contribute to the work of the Kingdom to their fullest potential. It is a product of conferences originally convened by Viva Network. The work will engage readers in a continuing conversation about God's heart for children. It identifies seven key statements which lay out the responsibility of the Church, families, and society toward children.

Marcia Bunge (ed). *The Child in Christian Thought* (Grand Rapids, Michigan: Eerdmans, 2001).

This book is a major survey of the history of Christian thought on children. Each chapter discusses perspectives held by influential theologians and Christian movements, and brings the benefit of each perspective to a sound contemporary view of childhood and child-rearing. It will prove a valuable resource for a Christian view of childhood and child-rearing today.

Scottie May, Beth Posterski, Catherine Stonehouse and Linda Cannell. *Children Matter: Celebrating Their Place in the Church, Family and Community* (Grand Rapids, Michigan: Eerdmans, 2005).

The Church should serve as a faith community where children can be welcomed, instructed, nurtured and recognized as a model of faith. This easy-read book examines biblical, theological, philosophical and developmental perspectives. A large portion is devoted to faith development of children. The final section offers practical suggestions for what the Church and families can do to nurture children's faith. It challenges readers to recognize, and live out the truth that children are an integral part of the Church and of Kingdom-building.

Ron Buckland. *Children and the Gospel* (Scripture Union Australia, 2001).

The leaders, preachers, poets and parents of 2050 are with us now – as children. *Children and the Gospel* affirms that our ministry among children and families has the potential to change our world; it encourages us to pursue excellence. The book contains a carefully-reasoned theological perspective and explores 20 principles which provide a framework for excellence. It is a useful tool for stimulating theological reflection and for assessing & improving existing ministry activity.

Training course: *Celebrating Children course.* Developed by Viva, in conjunction with key international child development specialists and practitioners. This 128-hour course combines a biblical basis, practical skills, and academic theory on child development. http://book.viva.org/civicrm/contribute/transact?reset=1&id=12

Websites for research, resources and training:

The Global Alliance for Advancing Holistic Child Development, http://hcd-alliance.org/

The Society for Children's Spirituality, http://childspirituality.org/

Viva: Together for Children, http://www.viva.org/

The Global Children's Forum, http://www.globalchildrensforum.com

The 4/14 Window Movement, http://4to14window.com/

The Child Theology Movement, http://www.childtheology.org

Max7 Open Source ministry resource library for leaders discipling children, http://www.max7.org/

World Vision Research (Basic Orientation Module on the Spiritual Nurture of Children, 2010 and Focus Group Discussion Project papers) and http://wvi.org/

Spiritual State of the World's Children, http://onehope.net/sswc/

PART 2 • SECTION IID-6
Evangelism and Prayer

J. Edwin Orr. *The Role of Prayer in Spiritual Awakening* (1977) Campus Crusade for Christ conference. Available on YouTube. http://www.youtube.com/watch?v=ixoQgVbVkNc

Presented by one of the most trusted historians on revival in the twentieth century, Orr tells story after story supporting the basic premise that 'There has never been a spiritual awakening in any county or locality that did not begin with united prayer.' One of the best ever lectures on this topic.

Tom White. *City-Wide Prayer Movements: One Church, Many Congregations* (Ventura, California. Regal Books, 2001).

Here is a practitioner's guide to help plant, develop, and sustain movements of increased unity, prayer, and collaboration in cities and regions, resulting in more evangelistic opportunities. White moves beyond the conceptual and theological, and offers in-the-trenches practical wisdom for multi-denominational city leadership teams working in movements that are emerging, gaining momentum or well established The appendix is particularly helpful, sharing insights for establishing city leadership teams, and getting a variety of kingdom assets in a city on the same page.

Ed Silvoso. *That None Should Perish: How to Reach Entire Cities for Christ Through Prayer Evangelism* (Ventura, California. Regal Books, 1994) and *Prayer Evangelism: How to Change the Spiritual Climate Over Your Home, Neighborhood and City* (Ventura, California. Regal Books, 2000).

These two books address prayer for personal evangelism, and prayer for evangelism in the entire community. Everyone will not agree with everything presented. Catch the heart and the big picture of the role of prayer in leading people into a relationship with the Savior.

Andrew Murray. *With Christ in the School of Prayer, A 31 Day Course on Christian Prayer.* Public Domain.

First published in 1887 but still available from several publishers in several formats, including electronic. Murray (1828-1917) offers a structured series of thirty-one practical and powerful lessons on prayer. Drawing on Scripture, he begins each day by showing how biblical principles apply to Christian prayer. Murray discusses the importance of the Holy Spirit in prayer and the value of faith, forgiveness, and perseverance. Each day's lesson ends with Andrew Murray sharing a personal prayer.

Paul Wemmer. *Count Zinzendorf and the Spirit of the Moravians* – Self published. Contact paul4120@gmail.com for more information.

Few people have had more impact upon the modern missionary endeavor than Zinzendorf. Anything written about him or by him will call you to a deeper love for 'the Lamb that was slain' and prayer. This work is recommended because Wemmer, who is fluent in both German and English, was able to live in the Moravian village of Herrnhut for over six months and had access to many original documents. Zinzendorf was overwhelmingly struck by the love of Jesus expressed by his wounds. This shaped everything he did. Out of this love came a deep commitment to live for Christ's glory. The prayers from the Moravian Movement spawned and supported missionary endeavors in many parts of the world. NB. The influence of Samuel Mills and his friends at Williams College, Massachusetts (see the Wikipedia entry to the 'Haystack prayer meeting, 1806') is also worth class study.

THE CAPE TOWN CALL TO ACTION

UNIT II

Part 2 • Section IIE-1, 3-5
Biblical Lifestyle
Distinctiveness / Humility; Integrity / Success; Simplicity / Greed

Henri Nouwen. *In the Name of Jesus: Reflections on Christian Leadership* (New York: The Crossroad Publishing Company, 1992).

J. Oswald Sanders. *Spiritual Leadership* (Chicago: Moody Press, 1994).

Jonathan Lamb. *Integrity* (Nottingham: IVP, 2007).

Henri Nouwen and J. Oswald Sanders, coming from different churchmanships, present classic treatments on the integrity of Christian leadership, both written with clarity, passion, and conviction. They touch upon issues of moral character, and point the leader towards an embodiment of Christ's humility, integrity, selflessness, surrender, and simplicity. Nouwen does so by taking the reader through the temptations of Jesus, showing how contemporary leaders face similar enticements, while Sanders compiles a list of Christ-like attributes that all leaders should emulate.

Jonathan Lamb, Director of Preaching at Langham Partnership, writes with a searching lucidity, using contemporary illustrations and modeling fine of use of scripture as he urges leaders to model integrity in their lives and dealings.

Richard J. Foster. *Celebration of Discipline: The Path to Spiritual Growth Third Edition* (San Francisco: Harper & Row, 1998).

Dallas Willard. *The Divine Conspiracy: Rediscovering Our Hidden Life with God* (San Francisco: Harper & Row, 1998).

Two more classic texts deal with interweaving themes of integrity, simplicity, and humility. Foster's work nurtures the Christian life within spiritual disciplines, mounting a formidable attack against the superficiality of modern societies. Willard focuses on the Sermon on the Mount, showing that God's nature forms the basis for human existence. In this study, he underscores how Christians are called to follow the way of Christ by surmounting evil with good.

Christopher J. H. Wright (ed). *Portrait of a Radical Disciple: Reflections of John Stott's Life and Ministry* (Downers Grove, Illinois: IVP, 2011). [IVP Nottingham title: *John Stott: A Portrait by his Friends*].

Chris Wright et al. *John Stott: Pastor, Leader and Friend* (*Didasko Files* series: Peabody, Massachusetts: Hendrickson Publishers / Lausanne Library, 2012).

Wright gathers personal tributes by some of John Stott's friends. Few subjects offer as compelling a picture of humility, integrity and simplicity. We see him as parish minister, author, global leader across the continents. The *Didasko File* includes sections on his role (i) in founding The Langham Partnership, (ii) as an evangelist to the student world, and (iii) as a leading figure in The Lausanne Movement.

Brother Lawrence. *The Practice of the Presence of God*. Edited and paraphrased by Donald E. Demaray (New York: Alba, 1997).

Thomas a Kempis. *The Imitation of Christ* (New York: Alba, 1996).

Dietrich Bonhoeffer. *The Cost of Discipleship* (New York: Collier, 1965).

The three books represent classics of the Christian faith. Each borrows from the life of Christ to engage in issues of Christian integrity, simplicity, or discipleship from within their relevant epoch in history, whether 14th century (a Kempis), 17th century (Brother Lawrence), or 20th century Europe (Bonhoeffer). The writings of these men deserve to be read, re-read, digested, and absorbed for the insights gained as they struggle with what it means to submit, and to worship through the whole of life, as they follow Christ with humility, integrity and simplicity.

Ronald J. Sider. *Rich Christians in an Age of Hunger: Moving From Affluence to Generosity* (Nashville: Thomas Nelson, 2005).

Jonathan J. Bonk. *Missions and Money: Affluence as a Missionary Problem.* Revised Expanded Edition. (New York: Orbis, 2007).

Duane Elmer. *Cross-Cultural Servanthood: Serving the World in Christlike Humility* (Downers Grove, Illinois: IVP, 2006).

John Howard Yoder. *The Politics of Jesus* (Grand Rapids, Michigan: Eerdmans, 1996).

These divergent-yet-similar works stand upon the conviction that the gospel be lived has social, economic, and political implications. Sider, Bonk, and Elmer wrestle with cross-cultural implications of Christian discipleship, calling upon Western churches to give serious contemplation to the ways they give, love, and serve others around the world. They raise their collective voice prophetically in the face of gluttony, greed, pride, and selfishness in our churches. Yoder contends that everything that Jesus did was of political importance, calling people to represent Christ by being peacemakers in society.

PART 2 • SECTION IIE-2
Sexuality

National Association of Evangelicals. *Theology of Sex* (2009). Booklet available for free download at http://naegeneration.com/resources

Stanton Jones. (January, 2011). 'How to teach sex: Seven realities Christians in every congregation need to know.' *Christianity Today*, pp. 34-39. Article available for free download at http://www.christianitytoday.com/ct/2011/january/34.34.html. See also http://www.Christiansexed.com, the website the Joneses have established as a resource for Christian parents pursuing biblically-grounded sex education in the home.

These two resources offer brief and accessible overviews of Christian perspectives on human sexuality at a general level. Both emphasize the creational goodness of sexuality, the brokenness that sin introduces, and the relevance and enduring authority of biblical teaching on sexual morality. The booklet, Theology of Sex is an initiative of the National Association of Evangelicals arising out of concern for the continuing prevalence of abortion in American society and the compromised effectiveness of the church in addressing sexual concerns. It is designed to be read by adult education classes, and includes helpful questions for discussion by church members and leaders. The Jones article is similar, and the website provides an array of helpful resources for Christian parents.

Dennis Hollinger. *The Meaning of Sex: Christian Ethics and the Moral Life* (Grand Rapids: Baker, 2009).

Dale Kuehne. *Sex and the iWorld: Rethinking Relationship Beyond an Age of Individualism* (Grand Rapids: Baker, 2009).

Hollinger and Kuehne are thoughtful contributions on human sexuality. Hollinger brings a more traditional, systematic treatment from biblical, theological, ethical, and pastoral perspectives, addressing complex ethical issues with compassion. Kuehne grapples with the same ethical and theological issues, from the perspective of cultural analysis. He portrays our current dilemmas as arising from a broad rejection of 'antiquated' views of sexuality (eg traditional male hierarchy) in favor of an individualistic and often hedonistic (and profoundly unbiblical) understanding of sexuality (the iWorld). Kuehne offers the alternative of a biblically-grounded relational ethic (the rWorld).

Mark Yarhouse. *Homosexuality and the Christian: A guide for parents, pastors and friends* (Minneapolis, Minneapolis: Bethany, 2010).

Richard Hays. 'Homosexuality' (Chapter 16) in *The Moral Vision of the New Testament* (San Francisco: HarperSanFrancisco, 1996).

Robert Gagnon. *The Bible and Homosexual Practice* (Nashville: Abingdon, 2001). See other Gagnon resources at http://www.robgagnon.net/

Stanton Jones. (2006). Study guide and response to Mel White's *What the Bible says—and doesn't say—about homosexuality*. Booklet available for free download at http://www.wheaton.edu/CACE/resources/booklets/StanJonesResponsetoMelWhite.pdf

These four resources offer different strengths in addressing homosexuality. Yarhouse is a comprehensive practical guide for those struggling with homosexual preference. It builds from a Christian perspective but is strongest on interpreting psychological and social scientific issues, lucidly and helpfully. The Hays chapter is a compassionate, biblically-grounded argument defending the traditional Christian position. Gagnon's book is the gold standard of comprehensive scholarly biblical research demonstrating that the Bible, properly understood, does indeed judge homosexual practice morally problematic; it is detailed but worth the effort. The Jones booklet is a readable response to the commonly-voiced arguments for affirmation of homosexuality by the self-identified Christian Mel White.

Part 2 • Section IIE-3
Power

Larry L. Rasmussen. 'Power Analysis: A Neglected Agenda in Christian Ethics.' In *The Annual of the Society of Christian Ethics* (ed). D.M. Yaeger, pp. 3-17. (Washington DC: The Society of Christian Ethics, 1991).

This article offers a guide to the eleven elements of complex power. Absence of power analysis among leaders of the church causes many conflicts. The author states that God is the source of power; therefore, the original purpose of power is to do good and not harm. Unless power is taken back to its intended function, neither the church nor missionary work will perform its purpose. The author affirms that right use of power is a permanent concern for ethics. The article explores how power in nature/society has already shaped lives theologically, before a person reflects on God. It also asks how differences in religious, self-understanding, and moral action may be grounded in differing experiences of power in home, community, school, church, nations.

Marguerite Shuster. *Power, Pathology, Paradox: The Dynamics of Evil and Good* (Grand Rapids, Michigan: Zondervan, 1987).

The book is divided into three sections: power, pathology, and paradox. The section on power shows how all human decisions are based on the concept of whether one has power. These decisions are made in response to the higher powers and principalities of the supernatural world. The section on pathology teaches that the dynamics of evil are found in the disruption of structure (due to human powerlessness) allowing Satan to insert himself into a person's weakness and will. Shuster explains that Christians must not combat Satan on his own terms or on his own turf, but through the Word and Spirit of God. One cannot negate or relinquish the reality and existence of evil in all realms of life (family, society, politics, organizations, religions, etc).

Clinton E. Arnold. *Power and Magic: The Concept of Power in Ephesians* (Eugene, Oregon: Wipf and Stock Publishers, 1989).

Power and Magic offers a study of the language of 'power' in Ephesians, including Christ's power over powers and authorities. Arnold presents an outline to comprehend spiritual power from a biblical point of view. Clinton surveys the religious practices and beliefs common in Asia Minor, particularly Gnosticism and the cult of Artemis. Clinton offers a brief history of the role of the spiritual powers in the New Testament, referring to scholars like Dibelius, Wink and Carr. Clinton relates the understanding of the powers to a strong Christology, and a theological grasp of election, humanity, the New Creation, eschatology, salvation, and ecclesiology. The author suggests that the background of Ephesians consists in (i) the churches of Asia Minor seeking guidance to craft a Christian perspective on the 'powers', and (ii) encouragement in their constant fights with the destructive spirit-forces.

Miroslav Volf. *After Our Likeness: The Church as the Image of the Trinity.* Sacra Doctrina: Christian Theology for a Postmodern Age (Series ed. Alan G. Padgett. Grand Rapids, Michigan: Eerdmans, 1998).

Different interpretations of the Trinity resulted in different styles of the use of power in church leadership. *After Our Likeness* compares the Episcopal models of ecclesiology endorsed by Ratzinger and Zizioulas, with the Catholic and Orthodox acceptance of a hierarchical form of polity. Volf projects the merits of his free-church theory, a proposal of a democratic and egalitarian style of organization. He states that Christians must learn to offset the tendencies toward Christomonism and individualism in ecclesiology, offering a social model in which all members are related to one another and to the Lord. The Trinitarian vision of the Church seeks to do justice to the person and the community. This book helps us to understand why every denomination has different views of power when reaching out to the communities. Volf brings theology and sociology together. He concludes clearly that the mission of the Church is not to gratify the tastes of religious consumers but to bear witness to the guidance of God exposed in Jesus Christ.

Robert Linthicum. *Transforming Power: Biblical Strategies for Making a Difference in Your Community* (Downers Grove, Illinois: IVP, 2003).

Linthicum does not refer to political power, but to the daily life power of bringing positive change to neighborhoods and cities. The book has two sections, the 'Theology of Power' and the 'Practice of Power.' In the first part, he lays out a biblical framework in which to place power. The author describes God's desire for a community of peace (*shalom*) and then looks to the human destruction of this community. The author mentions several biblical examples in the early church through the apostles where relational power is used in positive ways. *Transforming Power* discusses the differences between relational power, legislative power, and violent power. It considers relational power to be the greatest, because Jesus used it to triumph over the corrupt legislative power during his time. In the second section, Linthicum offers principles and practical strategies for utilizing power to bring about transformation. The book emphasizes that power, when used properly as delegated authority, causes a healthy growth and freedom.

Additional Resources:

Chris Frilingos. 'For My Child, Onesimus: Paul and Domestic Power in Philemon' *Journal of Biblical Literature* 119, no. 1 (2000): pp. 91-104.

Larry B. Jones. 'The Problem of Power in Ministry Relationships' *Evangelical Missions Quarterly* 45, no. 4 (2009): pp. 404-410.

Walter Wink. *Naming the Powers: The Language of Power in the New Testament.* Powers. 3 vols. Vol. 1 (Philadelphia: Fortress Press, 1984-1992).

Philip B. Payne. "Biblical Foundation for Mutual Submission and Shared Authority Between Men and Women in Church and Marriage," 2011. CD, DVD and MP3 available through http://www.equalitydepot.com

Alan Padgett. *As Christ Submits to the Church: A Biblical Understanding of Leadership and Mutual Submission* (Grand Rapids: Baker Academic, 2011).

Aida Besancon Spencer and William David Spencer. "What Makes A Marriage Work," 2009. CD, DVD and MP3 available through http://www.equalitydepot.com

Payne surveys the exegetical, theological, and practical foundations for mutuality between men and women in Scripture and responds to the primary objections to biblical mutuality. Padgett contends that as Christ came to serve the church, so all Christians must serve and care for one other; he explores Christ-like leadership and the practical outworkings of mutual submission in the church today. Married theologians Spencer and Spencer discuss 25 biblical principles for a successful marriage based on their 37 years of marriage.

Manfred T. Brauch. "Transformation of Relationships: The Biblical Subversion of the Nature and Exercise of Power," 2011. CD available through http://www.equalitydepot.org

MaryKate Morse. *Making Room for Leadership: Power, Space and Influence* (Downers Grove: InterVarsity Press, 2008).

Gilbert Bilezikian. *Community 101: Reclaiming the Church as a Community of Oneness* (Grand Rapids: Zondervan, 1997).

Brauch examines human relationships and communities in light of the exercise of power, and explores how the life and teachings of Jesus challenge human power relationships, including gender relationships. Morse looks at Christ's use of power as a guide for how to lead in ways that are empowering to others, including women. Bilezikian contends that the local church is to be a community in which all believers are equal before Christ and analyzes the roles and responsibilities of leadership.

Catherine Clark Kroeger, Nancy Nason-Clark, and Barbara Fisher-Townsend (eds). *Beyond Abuse in the Christian Home: Raising Voices for Change* (Eugene: Wipf and Stock Publishers, 2008).

Medad Birungi. "Gender Injustice Destroys the Whole Family: One Child's Experience," 2007. PDF available through http://www.equalitydepot.org

Jane McNally and Alvera Mickelson. *Abuse and Remedy: The Abuse of Christian Women in India and 12 Studies on Biblical Equality* (Pasadena: William Carey Library, 2005).

The above resources address the issue for the end of any kind of abuse in marriage. Kroeger et al have compiled a collection of articles on confronting abuse in Christian homes. Birungi, a university teacher in his native Uganda, describes his father's abuse of himself, his siblings, and his mother and calls for an end to domestic violence in his country. McNally, a forty-year missionary to India, and Mickelsen discuss the abuse of women in Christian homes in India and provide scriptural teachings on the matter.

The following secular sociology books serve well in understanding 'power.'

Richard Newbold Adams. *Energy and Structure: A Theory of Social Power* (Austin: University of Texas Press, 1975), 100-173.

Michael Foucault. *Power/Knowledge: Selected Interviews and Other Writings 1972-1977* (ed). Colin Gordon (New York: Pantheon Books, 1980).

PART 2 • SECTION IIE-5
Generosity (Simplicity in Lifestyle)

Brett Elder and Stephen Grabill (eds). *NIV Stewardship Study Bible: Discover God's design for life, the environment, finances, generosity and eternity* (Grand Rapids: Zondervan, 2009).

> Perhaps the definitive resource for understanding biblical generosity and stewardship, the *Stewardship Study Bible* unpacks the biblical understanding of stewardship in a deep way. With its 366 Exploring stewardship notes, text notes on stewardship, Crown Financial Ministries' Biblical Index on Money and Possessions and 30-Day Journey towards Generous Living, it explains the privilege Christians have to manage what God has given to them and live generous lives. A helpful library resource for theological institutions and churches, the *Stewardship Study Bible* is also a rich basis for curriculum development and for teaching.

John Stott. *The Grace of Giving: 10 Principles of Christian Giving* (*Didasko Files* series. Peabody, Massachusetts: Hendrickson Publishers / Lausanne Library 2012).

Arif Mohamed, Brett Elder and Stephen Grabill (eds). *Kingdom Stewardship: Occasional Papers prepared by the Lausanne Resource Mobilization Working Group for Cape Town 2010* (Grand Rapids: Christian Library Press, 2010).

Generosity Declaration, http://generositymovement.org/network/ and *Global Generosity*

Network Affirmations, http://generositymovement.org/about/

Lausanne Standards, http://www.lausannestandards.org

> Based on an exposition of 2 Corinthians 8 and 9, John Stott's tight and lucid 24pp *Didasko File* helps Christians think more purposefully about the way they use their resources. *Kingdom Stewardship* is a compilation of essays on stewardship and generosity written by authors from around the world. It challenges the global church to a culture of Christian generosity and wise stewardship in support of global mission. *The Generosity Declaration* is drafted by The Lausanne Movement / World Evangelical Alliance Global Generosity Network. Christian bodies and individuals can sign the Declaration as their commitment to a generous lifestyle. The Global Generosity Network Affirmations is a summary of biblical generosity principles while the *Lausanne Standards* are affirmations and agreements on the giving and receiving of money in mission.

Wesley K. Willmer (ed). *Revolution in Generosity: Transforming Stewards to Be Rich Toward God* (Chicago: Moody Publishers, 2008).

Ron Sider. *Just Generosity* (Grand Rapids: Baker Books, 2007).

Randy Alcorn. *The Treasure Principle: Unlocking the secret of joyful giving* (Colorado Springs: Multnomah Books, 2001).

Dennis Tongoi. *Mixing God with Money: Strategies for living in an uncertain economy* (Nairobi, Kenya: Bezalel Investment Ltd, 2001).

John L Ronsvalle and Sylvia Ronsvalle. *The State of Church Giving Through 2009: Jesus Christ, the Church in the U.S., & the 16 No-Progress-in-Child Deaths Nations, 10 Being 84% Christian* (Chicago: Empty Tomb, 2011).

> Amongst a number of very good books on generosity, these books are perhaps the most important. Some of the best generosity scholars, leaders, practitioners and thinkers reflect on money from God's perspective in *Revolution in Generosity*, making it an essential resource for teaching on generosity. Ron Sider shows in *Just Generosity* how generous evangelical Christians can overcome poverty in the United States. Translated into 20 languages, *The Treasure Principle* is possibly the most widely-used generosity resource in the world. With its study guide and video, it is ideal for use in small groups and churches. Dennis Tongoi's *Mixing God with Money* looks at generous living from within the African context. This makes his book distinctive, as an example of what is needed in contexts outside the West. John and Sylvia Ronsvalle give what can be a disturbing picture of church giving in the US in 2009 in the 21st edition of *The State of Church Giving*.

Video: 'Life is Gift', 'Grace of Giving' and 'Handful of Rice'

Three videos from the US, Uganda and India that look at generosity as a life of giving, as transforming communities and as supporting mission. There are also other generosity resources on the website.
http://generositymovement.org/category/resources/videos/

Video: Various generosity teaching videos are available through the Generous Church website
http://www.generouschurch.com/videos

The Generous Giving Library is the best place to find generosity related articles, sermons and teaching material.
http://library.generousgiving.org/page.asp?sec=28&page=

ilikegiving.com is a website with videos of daily giving stories.
http://ilikegiving.com/

'40 Day Journey to a More Generous Life', Bible Devotional by Brian Kluth (available digitally in 40+ languages)
http://www. MAXIMUMgenerosity.org

We offer the following generosity-related websites:

http://www.generousgiving.org
http://www.generouschurch.com
http://www.MAXIMUMgenerosity.org
http://www.stewardship.org.uk
http://maclellan.net/generosity
http://www.generositymovement.org
http://www.intsteward.org
http://www.stewardshipcouncil.net
http://www.nationalchristian.com
http://www.generouslife.org
http://www.crown.org
http://www.christianstewardshipnetwork.com
http://www.epm.org/resources/category/money-and-giving/
http://www.stewardshipministries.org
http://www.revolutioningenerosity.com/resources.html
http://www.givingwisely.com

A compilation of generosity videos, a generosity reader, generosity articles, generosity presentations and papers, generosity information and generosity books in pdf format. This DVD can be obtained from Dr Sas Conradie at
http://sas.conradie@cms-uk.org

Generosity facilitators in the US who can assist in teaching and speaking on generosity:

Dr Stephen Grabill (sgrabill@acton.org), Brett Elder (belder@acton.org), Daryl Heald (darylheald@gmail.com), Dave Wills (dwills@nationalchristian.com), Todd Peterson (tpeterson@givingwisely.com), Michael Pepper (mpepper@givingwisely.com), Dr Brian Kluth (bk@kluth.org), Mike Schneider (mike@ministryspotlight.org), Henry Kaestner (hkaestner@bandwidth.com), Rob Martin (rob@firstfruit.org), Patrick Johnson (patrick@generouschurch.com)

For more resources in this area, see above, Part 2 Section II E 5, 1, 3-5 on Biblical Lifestyle.

THE CAPE TOWN CALL TO ACTION

UNIT 12

PART 2 • SECTION IIF-1
Unity and Partnership in Global Mission

Samuel Escobar. 'Evangelical Missiology: peering into the future at the turn of the century.' in William Taylor (ed). *Global Missiology for the 21st century* pp.109-110 (Grand Rapids, Michigan: Baker Academic, 2000).

The South American missiologist Samuel Escobar criticizes contemporary mission strategies, and particularly those from the West, for turning missions into management models. There is too much emphasis on results, and too little attention to the spiritual essence of mission. There is an over-reliance on social science theories, and far from enough respect for God's sovereignty. Escobar presents a refreshing perspective on global mission. A stimulating article on how the Church from the West and the majority world should be learning from one another for global mission.

Patrick Fung. 'Partnership in the body of Christ toward a new global equilibrium', *Cape Town 2010 Advance Papers*.

Patrick Fung, General Director of OMF International, challenged the title 'toward a new global equilibrium': 'Equilibrium will never eliminate comparison and competition. However, unity with one heart and mind under the Lordship of Christ will bring about a sacrificial sharing of God's resources for world evangelization.' Fung suggested that the biblical model of Christian partnership is not a 'win-win' model, in the way the world promotes, but always sacrificial on both sides. No one ethnic group or nation can claim the exclusive privilege of being the ones to finish the Great Commission. Arrogance and self-pity will be the major barriers to pursuing world evangelization. Also, the author proposed there is a desperate need for more missiological thinking beyond the Western paradigm which speaks to the contemporary political, social, religious and ethnic contexts.

Hwa Yung. 'Kingdom Identity in Christian Mission' *Mission Round Table - The Occasional Bulletin of OMF Mission Research*, Vol. 4 (2) December 2008: pp. 2-11.

Bishop Hwa Yung, of the Methodist Church in Malaysia, shows how a true discovery / recovery of Christian identity makes missionary effort effective and fruitful. He urges that an indigenous church develop a clear self-understanding, not merely borrowing from a church of another culture. Under the leading of the Holy Spirit and in the light of Scriptures, the church will then address issues arising from its own context, and begin to define its own understanding of the Christian faith in terms and language drawn from its own cultural categories and thought patterns. The author uses examples from China, Africa and India to illustrate the importance of biblical, indigenous Christian thinking and practice.

Steve S. Moon and David Tai-Woong Lee. 'Globalization, world evangelization, and global missiology' in Richard Tiplady (ed) *One World or Many* (Pasadena, California: William Carey Library, 2003).

One World or Many brings contributions from diverse cultural and ethnic backgrounds, all with a common commitment to biblical truth and a passion for global evangelization. Steve Moon and David Lee, both Korean with rich experience in the West, argue for an urgent new missiology to fit a new global context. The global missionary community needs to produce this new missiology. They argue (i) for a creative tension between 'globality' and 'contextuality'; and (ii) that 'missiology' must be context-driven, and strive for biblical wholeness.

Andrew Walls. 'Christian Mission in a Five-hundred-year Context' in Andrew Walls and Cathy Ross (eds) *Mission in the 21st Century - Exploring the 5 Marks of Global Mission* (Maryknoll, New York: Orbis, 2008).

Andrew Walls, scholar and historian in mission and church history, who coined the term 'Mission from anywhere to anywhere' was once described by *Christianity Today* as an historian 'ahead of his time'. He observed, 'In the multi-centric Christian church there can be no automatic assumption of Western leadership; indeed, if suffering and endurance are the badges of authenticity, we can expect the most powerful Christian leadership to come from elsewhere.'

While scholars such as Philip Jenkins emphasize a shift of power from Western churches to those south of the equator, Walls sees a new polycentrism: the riches of a hundred places learning from each other. Walls, who gained rich experience as a mission practitioner in Africa, challenges churches from the West, the East and the global South to learn from one another for global mission

'Mobilization and the growing Asian Missionary Movement', *Mission Round Table - The Occasional OMF Bulletin of Mission Research*, April 2006, Vol. 2 (1).

This special issue from the *Mission Round Table* focuses on mission mobilization in the context of growing Asian Mission Movements. Kang San Tan, the editor and an Asian missiologist, highlighted how he was uncomfortable with the term, 'mission mobilization'. *First*, it comes from the military image of mobilizing forces to war. It conjures concepts of a task, a responsibility, rather than participation in God's work. *Second*, it belongs to the old paradigm of mobilizing resources from Western countries to the rest of the world; from the haves to the have nots. This issue also looks at some of the implications for Western mission agencies in responding to newer sending communities such as the Asian Missionary Movements. *Mission Round Table* is a publication by OMF International, a mission agency focusing on evangelization among East Asia's peoples.

PART 2 • SECTION IIF-2
Partnership in Christian Mission

Lausanne Covenant (1974): http://www.lausanne.org/en/documents/lausanne-covenant.html

Manila Manifesto (1989): http://www.lausanne.org/en/component/content/article.html?id=87

Cape Town Commitment (2010): http://www.lausanne.org/en/documents/ctcommitment.html#p2-6

Partnership in Christian mission has been an integral theme of The Lausanne Movement since the beginning. Two sections of *The Lausanne Covenant* (sections #7 & #8) were dedicated to partnership. Likewise, in *The Manila Manifesto*, one of the major affirmations (#17) and one of the core sections (#9) were dedicated to partnership. And *The Cape Town Commitment* also includes multiple affirmations of partnership in Christian mission (Specifically, Part 1 / Section 9a and Part 2 / Sections 6.1 & 6.2).

The foundational theology of partnership in Christian mission rests on *unity* and *diversity*. The theme of unity is obviously prevalent in the Scriptures - from the oneness of the Trinity, to the fellowship of Christians, to the constant appeals for Christians to 'love one another' and to be 'of one mind and spirit.' Jesus himself prayed that his followers would 'be one' as he and the Father were one, 'so that the world may believe' (John 17:20-23). And he said to his followers, 'By this everyone will know that you are my disciples, if you love one another' (John 13:35).

But the theme of diversity is equally present in the Scriptures through many descriptions of the varying roles, gifts, and functions in ministry (Romans 12, Ephesians 4, 1 Corinthians 12, Hebrews 2:4, John 4:35-38, 1 Corinthians 3:1-9, Hebrews 11:39-40). The Scriptures say that one plants while another waters and one sows while another reaps, 'so that the sower and the reaper may be glad together' (John 4:35-38).

God values unity, but not uniformity. God values diversity, but not division. True partnership is not simply a matter of equality. It is a matter of synergy. The Holy Spirit distributes differing gifts 'according to his will' (Hebrews 2:4) and it is through this functional diversity in the context of relational unity that God intends to accomplish his purposes in the world, 'so that in all things God may be praised through Jesus Christ' (1 Peter 4:7-11).

There is a strong biblical basis for partnership. It is a practical topic and not just a matter for theological discussion. For that reason, many resources recommended here emphasize the 'hands-on' / 'how-to' aspects of what it takes to form a viable, healthy, and effective partnership for mission.

Phill Butler. *Well Connected: Releasing Power, Restoring Hope through Kingdom Partnerships* (Colorado Springs, Colorado: Authentic, 2005).

Ernie Addicott. *Body Matters: A Guide to Partnership in Christian Mission* (Edmonds, Washington: IPA, 2005).

Daniel Rickett. *Making Your Partnership Work* (Enumclaw, Washington: WinePress, 2002).

These three books are some of the most practical resources available on the topic of partnership in Christian mission. These are 'must read' books.

Butler's book, *Well Connected*, is the most comprehensive in content. The late Ralph Winter, founder of the U.S. Center for World Mission, referred to it as 'the quintessential partnership handbook'. Drawing upon nearly 30 years of international partnership development experience with InterDev and visionSynergy, Butler writes for an audience of reflective practitioners who want to understand the 'why' of partnership development as well as the 'how' of partnering well. The first part develops the theological aspects of partnership, while the remainder provides a clearly-defined process for partnership development and a detailed description of the key factors for success. Drawing from significant personal experience, Butler includes dozens of real-world illustrations and abbreviated case studies.

Addicott's book, *Body Matters*, provides a very readable introduction to partnership in Christian mission. Addicott and Butler were colleagues at InterDev, so both books present the same process for partnership development - more condensed in Addicott's book. Addicott provides more in-depth discussion on the topics of cross-cultural differences and conflict management within inter-organizational partnerships. The book centers on the theme of relational health in the context of missional partnerships and makes the clear point that partnership is not just about the 'mechanics' of working together; it is fundamentally about trust.

Rickett's book, *Making Your Partnership Work*, is the earliest and most condensed of the three. It is organized around the three 'imperatives of partnership': vision, relationships, and results. Rickett writes in the introduction: 'To have productive partnerships, we must have vision, relationship, and results. Reduce a partnership to vision only, and it becomes no more than good intentions. Reduce it to relationship, and it becomes a fellowship without a purpose. Reduce it to results, and it loses its capacity to remain faithful. Vision, relationships, and results depend on one another for wholeness. They are interwoven in partnership and in ministry at its best' (p.23). Rickett includes useful resources and checklists to help readers evaluate the potential fit between partners, develop a common understanding, and evaluate the partnership itself.

Werner Mishke. *The Beauty of Partnership* (Scottsdale, Arizona: MissionONE, 2010).

Beth Birmingham & Scott Todd (eds). *Shared Strength: Exploring Cross-Cultural Christian Partnerships* (Compassion International, 2010).

Mary Lederleitner. *Cross-Cultural Partnerships: Navigating the Complexities of Money and Mission* (Downers Grove, Illinois: IVP, 2010).

The books by Mishke, Birmingham, Todd, and Lederleiter address key issues in cross-cultural partnerships such as equality, dependency and accountability *etc* in the global mission context, as the center of gravity continues to shift from established Western mission outreaches to majority-world ministries. Mishke's workbook helps readers understand essential components of healthy cross-cultural partnerships.

Birmingham and Todd provide a collection of articles addressing topics more-specifically focused in the area of relief and development.

Lederleiter's book directly addresses the highly-charged issue of money and partnership.

Rick Rusaw & Eric Swanson. *The Externally Focused Church* (Loveland, Colorado: Group, 2004).

Chip Sweney. *A New Kind of Big: How Churches of Any Size can Partner to Transform Communities* (Grand Rapids, Michigan: Baker, 2011).

There is great untapped potential for collaboration in local churches working together to reach and transform cities. The two books in this group provide practical introductions to local church partnerships and large-scale church/community partnerships which could bring dramatic impact in rapidly-expanding cities of the world.

Luis Bush & Lorry Lutz. *Partnering in Ministry: The Direction of World Evangelism* (Downers Grove, Illinois: IVP, 1990).

James Kraakevik & Dotsey Welliver (eds). *Partners in the Gospel: The Strategic Role of Partnership in World Evangelization* (Wheaton, Illinois: Billy Graham Center, 1991).

William Taylor (ed). *Kingdom Partnerships for Synergy in Missions* (Pasadena, California: William Carey, 1994).

The 1980s and 1990s saw a growing interest in partnerships for world evangelization. Hundreds of multi-lateral and international partnerships were launched with emphases on specific language groups, people groups, cities, regions, or countries of the world. The three books in this group provide a broad introduction to the field of collaboration in Christian mission, from the early days of the modern partnership movement. They cover a wide variety of topics and include a number of case-study models of partnership from around the world.

Mark Oxbrow. *'Better Together: Partnership and Collaboration in Mission'* (Edinburgh 2010. Conference Paper). Available at http://edinburgh2010.oikoumene.org/fileadmin/files/edinburgh2010/files/docs/Partnership%20.doc

Enoch Wan & Kevin Penman. *'The Why, How, and Who of Partnership in Christian Missions'* (2010). Available at http://ojs.globalmissiology.org/index.php/english/article/view/61

These articles are only two of numerous recent articles drawing on the wisdom of the last 20+ years of partnership practice in Christian mission. They are notable for their comprehensive perspective as they reflect on the recent history of partnership in mission and review some of the foundational literature on mission partnerships (including a number of the resources in this recommended list). Oxbrow aptly concludes his article with these words: 'We live in a networked world, our God exists in Trinitarian partnership, and God's mission into which we are drawn is inevitably characterized by collaboration and partnership …'

Videos: http://youtube.com/visionsynergy

visionSynergy's YouTube channel contains a growing library of story videos drawn from interviews with experienced ministry leaders from around the world who share their personal insights on the practice of partnership in Christian mission.

PART 2 • SECTION IIF-3
Men and Women in Partnership

The Cape Town Commitment upholds Lausanne's historic position that the partnership of men and women in evangelization 'must be welcomed for the common good' (Part 2, Section F-3A). It acknowledges the contributions of women to world missions, and The Third Lausanne Congress itself was produced with women in some of the central leadership and platform roles. The *Commitment* recognizes that different views are held on the partnership of men and women, and calls upon those on different sides of the debate to accept one another, without condemnation, and to study Scripture carefully together on the matter. The following bibliography reflects various voices in this conversation. Multiple contributors have recommended different resources, all of which have been noted:

James Beck (ed). *Two Views on Women in Ministry* (Grand Rapids: Zondervan, 2005).

Beck has clear and thorough articles, covering the spectrum of positions on the roles of men and women. Craig Keener and Linda Belleville endorse a full range of women's involvement in ministry; Craig Blomberg presents the view that women should be encouraged to fill any office or ministry other than elder; and Tom Schreiner that women should not teach or have authority over men. The four authors interact with each other in helpful dialogue.

Ward and Laurel Gasque. 'An Interview with F.F. Bruce', *St. Mark's Review*, 139, Spring 1989, pp. 4-10. Available for free download at http://www.theologicalstudies.org.uk/pdf/ffb/interview_bruce.pdf

Walter C. Kaiser, Jr. 'Correcting Caricatures: The Biblical Teaching on Women,' *Priscilla Papers*, Vol. 19:2, Spring 2005. Available for free download (pp. 1-4) at http://www.walterckaiserjr.com/women.html

Philip Barton Payne. *Man and Woman, One in Christ* (Grand Rapids: Zondervan, 2009).

Aida Besancon Spencer. *Beyond the Curse: Women Called to Ministry* (Peabody: Hendrickson, 1989).

In these resources, evangelical scholars examine the issue of biblical equality and whether women should be restricted in ministry due to their gender. In the Gasque interview, F.F. Bruce (author of commentaries on every epistle of Paul and the book of Acts) states that Paul's writings do not limit women's roles in leadership and teaching in the church. Kaiser concludes that in Genesis 2:18 women were created 'as a power corresponding to the man' and examines biblical passages sometimes used to limit the ministry of women, concluding that they do not do so. Payne contends, after decades of research, that Paul's theology, instruction, and practice consistently affirmed the equal standing of women in life and ministry. Spencer describes God's mandates for the partnership between men and women based on Genesis, Jesus, and Paul; an afterword by her husband, a pastor, gives practical commentary for shared partnership.

John Piper and Wayne Grudem. *Recovering Biblical Manhood and Womanhood: A Response to Evangelical Feminism* (Wheaton: Crossway, 2006).

Council for Biblical Manhood and Womanhood: http://www.cbmw.org

Ronald W. Pierce and Rebecca Merrill Groothuis (eds). *Discovering Biblical Equality: Complementarity Without Hierarchy* (Downers Grove: IVP, 2005).

Christians for Biblical Equality: http://www.cbeinternational.org/

These two books and their corresponding websites present and defend the more limited and broader involvement of women in ministry respectively. The articles cover historical, biblical, theological, hermeneutical and practical issues. Both have introductory essays outlining the issues. Each work concludes with suggestions for application in church and ministry. They are supported by their corresponding web sites. These offer a wide range of online books, specialized studies, articles, and book reviews. Pierce, Groothuis, and Fee have assembled twenty-six evangelical scholars who explore historical, biblical, theological, hermeneutical, and practical issues for biblical equality and partnership without a hierarchy of gender-based roles.

Robert Saucy and Judith TenElshof. *Women and Men in Ministry: A Complementary Perspective* (Chicago: Moody, 2001).

Andreas Kostenberger and Tom Schriener. *Women in the Church: An Analysis and Application of 1 Timothy 2:9-15* (Grand Rapids: Baker Academic, 2005).

Andreas Kostenberger and David Jones. *God, Marriage, and Family: Rebuilding the Biblical Foundation* (Wheaton: Crossway, 2010).

Debbie Dodd (ed). 'Women's Ministry Roles and Ordination Study Packet' article available for free download at http://breshears.net/?page_id=901

Sharon James. *God's Design for Women* (Darlington, UK: Evangelical Press. With study guide, 2007).

Saucy and TenElshof argue that women may serve in key areas of leadership, but not as elders. After essays on biblical themes, they discuss gender identity and roles, and conclude with application to church ministry. Kostenberger and Schreiner base their study of syntactical and exegetical observations on 1 Timothy 2:9-15. They argue that the passage prohibits women from authority positions in the church, and specifically from eldership. They apply the principles to a range of church and cultural issues. Kostenberger and Jones develop the view of male leadership in the church, home, marriage and family. They move on to discuss issues such as the theology of sex, parenting and divorce. Dodd's study is briefer and easily accessible, beginning with points of agreement on crucial definitions, position statements, and a discussion of licensure versus ordination. James reasons from scripture and from models of the home and marriage for the complementarian position. The combination of her keen mind and the accompanying study guide, commend this work for class discussion or for individual study.

Alan F. Johnson (ed). *How I Changed My Mind about Women in Leadership: Compelling Stories from Prominent Evangelicals* (Grand Rapids: Zondervan, 2010).

Evangelical leaders from a broad range of denominational affiliations and ethnic diversity share how they changed from a restrictive view about women in leadership to an inclusive view that recognizes a full shared partnership of leadership in the home and church based on gifting rather than gender.

Kenneth Bailey. *Paul Through Middle Eastern Eyes: Cultural Studies in 1 Corinthians* (Downers Grove: IVP, 2011).

Janette Hassey. *No Time for Silence: Evangelical Women in Public Ministry Around the Turn of the Century* (Minneapolis: Christians for Biblical Equality, 2008).

Loren Cunningham and David Hamilton with Janice Rogers. *Why Not Women: A Fresh Look at Scripture on Women in Missions, Ministry, and Leadership* (Seattle: YWAM Publishing, 2000).

These three resources all include an historical bent for understanding the scriptural foundations for biblical equality and the ministry of women. Bailey draws on his forty years of living and teaching New Testament in Egypt, Lebanon, Jerusalem, and Cyprus to render familiar passages back into their ancient setting, giving fresh insight on key passages about women. Hassey describes mid-nineteenth century women who taught at Bible institutes, preached at Bible conferences, served at local church pastorates, evangelized, and lead revivals over a hundred years ago. Cunningham, Hamilton, and Rogers provide an easily-readable survey of the scripture passages about women, a description of cultural factors that influenced the treatment of women in Jesus' day, and strong comments in support of women in ministry and leadership.

Richard Howell. 'How Hierarchy Leads to Abuse,' CD and DVD available at http://equalitydepot.com:80/howhierarchyleadstoabuse.aspx

Howell, an evangelical scholar from India, contends that cultures of hierarchy (i) maintain authority by claiming ontological distinction, (ii) conflict directly with ontological equality, and (iii) perpetuate abuse. He also discusses a biblical response to dominance.

Alvera Mickelson (ed). Lausanne Occasional Paper #53, 'Empowering Women and Men to Use their Gifts Together in Advancing the Gospel.' Published in *A New Vision, A New Heart, A Renewed Call, Volume II, Lausanne Occasional Papers from the 2004 Forum for World Evangelization in Pattaya, Thailand* (Pasadena: William Carey Library, 2005). The Occasional Paper is also available for free download at http://www.lausanne.org/documents/2004forum/LOP53_IG24.pdf

This Lausanne Occasional Paper offers a compilation of articles by international delegates to the Lausanne Forum in Pattaya, Thailand, in 2004 from Asia, Africa, Australia, Europe, North America, and South America. The Preface, 'Lausanne and Gender' reviews Lausanne's key statements on women in ministry in *The Lausanne Covenant* and *The Manila Manifesto*.

PART 2 • SECTION IIF-4
Theological Education and Mission

(i) The Call of the Church to Theological Education

Gary Parrett and Steven Kang. *Teaching the Faith, Forming the Faithful: A Biblical Mission for Education in the Church* (Downers Grove, Illinois: IVP, 2009).

Robert Pazmino. *Foundational Issues in Christian Education* (Grand Rapids: Baker Academic, 2008).

James R. Estep, Jr., Michael Anthony and Gregg Allison. *A Theology for Christian Education* (Nashville, B & H Publishing Co., 2008).

These three resources provide an excellent foundation for the role of the church in catechesis and the centrality of this task in its mission. These texts are all thoroughly rooted in a commitment to the Bible as God's Word, the centrality of Christ, and the sufficiency of the gospel to save. They demonstrate that the *paradosis* or 'passing down' of the faith implies more than simplistic formulas or popular phrases, but a thoroughgoing understanding of the faith and what it means to be a disciple of Jesus Christ. The church must be committed to theological education. This kind of missional discipleship begins in the home, is the lifeblood of the church and is supported by the specialized work of institutions in theological instruction. Parrett and Kang is particularly valuable because it sets forth a prescriptive plan for addressing the decline in catechesis.

(ii) The Missional Nature of Theological Education

Robert J. Banks. *Re-envisioning Theological Education: Exploring a Missional Alternative to Current Models* (Grand Rapids, Michigan: Eerdmans, 1999).

Linda Cannell. *Theological Education Matters: Leadership Education for the Church* (Newburgh, Indianapolis: EDCOT Press, 2006).

Edward Farley. *Theologia: The Fragmentation and Unity in Theological Education* (Wipf and Stock Publishers, 2001).

The Cape Town Commitment affirms that 'theological education is intrinsically missional.' However, increasingly theological education has become self-referential and non-missional. These three resources demonstrate the history of this problem and how it can be addressed Farley is especially important for its exposure to how theological education has become fragmented into separate disciplines and needs a deeper, unifying vision.

(iii) Theological Education and the Emergence of Global Christianity

Kwame Bediako. *Christianity in Africa: The Renewal of a Non-Western Religion* (Maryknoll, New York: Orbis Books, 1995).

Michael Goheen. *A Light to the Nations: The Missional Church and the Biblical Story* (Grand Rapids: Baker Academic, 2011).

Craig Ott and Harold A. Netland (eds). *Globalizing Theology: Belief and Practice in an Era of World Christianity* (Grand Rapids: Baker Academic, 2006).

Timothy C. Tennent. *Theology in the Context of World Christianity: How the Global Church is Influencing the Way We Think about and Discuss Theology* (Grand Rapids: Zondervan, 2007).

John Mbiti. 'Theological Impotence and the Universality of the Church,' 6-18 in Mission Trends, vol.3: *Third World Theologies*, Gerald H. Anderson and Thomas F. Stransky, eds. (New York: Paulist; Grand Rapids, Michigan: Eerdmans, 1990).

Andrew Walls. *The Missionary Movement in Christian History: Studies in the Transmission of the Faith* (Maryknoll, New York: Orbis Books and Edinburgh: T & T Clark, 1996). The first six chapters are especially crucial to this theme.

The growth of the Church in the non-western world brings implications for theological education. Bediako and Walls demonstrate how theological education had become captive to western agendas. The new era of the global church is (i) re-discovering Christianity as a non-western faith in all its vibrancy; (ii) seeing the western church being renewed through this discovery; (iii) transforming Theological education through this global encounter.

Tennent and Mbiti set forth the way in which systematic theology is being transformed by the emergence of global Christianity. Netland and Ott provide an excellent collection of essays which shows how the methods of theological education are being transformed by the global church. Finally, Goheen reminds us of the missional nature of the church and how theological education is part and parcel of this vision.

www.ingramcontent.com/pod-product-compliance
Lightning Source LLC
Chambersburg PA
CBHW080559090426
42735CB00016B/3290